'I still have my Sterling No.3
notebook and pencil from that
portentous day in 1957 when I
hung around Gloucester Central
and Eastgate stations, taking
in the smell of smoke, steam
and oil ... I was hooked!'

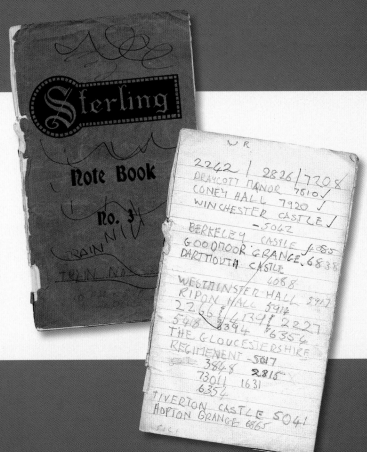

JULIAN HOLLAND

Railway Top Spots

David and Charles

Contents

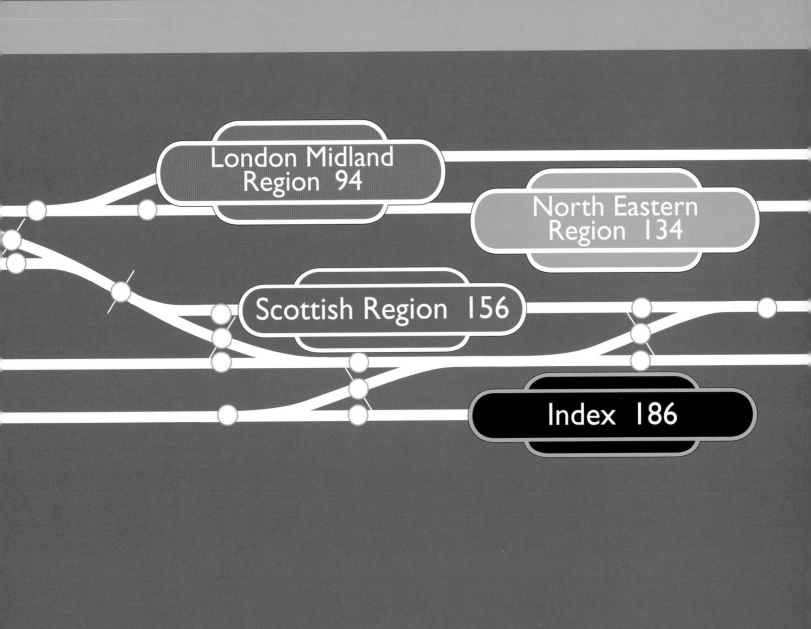

Introduction

Some very rude things have been said by some very ignorant people about trainspotters and I'm not having it!

▲ Our young budding trainspotter at the controls of a miniature steam locomotive at Exmouth in 1954.

No, I didn't eat fish paste sandwiches or even wear an anorak! For me it was a wonderful all-consuming hobby during my teenage years and although the writing down of locomotive numbers might seem to be very boring to the uninitiated, to me it was much more than just that. In pursuit of my hobby I travelled far and wide from my home town of Gloucester, usually with likeminded school chums, visiting obscure and often remote railway stations and engine sheds – every trip was an adventure and my knowledge of the geography of our country has stood me in good stead ever since. The evocative sights, sounds and smells of our much maligned state railways will remain embedded in my memory until my dying day.

My trainspotting trips were funded not only by pocket money but also by canny saving of my five shillings a week school dinner money – back in the early 1960s the cost of travelling by train was a highly regulated affair with fares being based purely on mileage although the wide availability of cheap day excursions at child prices made a trip to Birmingham, London or beyond very manageable even with my own meagre funds. Owning a bike was essential for more local trips – one of my favourite haunts on a summer Saturday was Churchdown station, midway between Gloucester and Cheltenham, where the steady stream of holiday trains (mainly steam hauled) from the North and the Midlands to the Southwest kept me transfixed with delight from early morning to early evening. During the school summer holidays I would often cycle to Swindon (a round trip of 60 miles) where the Locomotive Works was open on Wednesdays for free guided tours – Bristol Temple Meads was also a good cycling destination. Bedtime reading was usually a Western Region timetable from which I would organise the most convoluted railway journeys in my mind!

Despite this gadding around, my trainspotting forays were still limited to days out and by 1963 I had decided to spread my wings. Amazing 'shed bashing' trips organised by the Warwickshire Railway Society allowed me to venture further afield – 23 steam sheds in South Wales on 7 April (admittedly by coach) and a fantastic trip to Scotland by train (hauled by No. 46256)

▼ Playing at trains – the extensive '0' Gauge clockwork model railway built by my father in the attic of our home in Gloucester.

► A daily scene on the ex-MR High Orchard branch to Gloucester Docks, located only 100 yards from my home. Here, ex-MR Class '0F' 0-4-0T No. 41535 hauls a train of imported Baltic timber alongside Gloucester Park and towards the level crossing across Parkend Road on its journey to Eastgate goods sidings.

LOCOMOTIVES

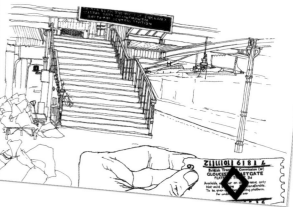

◀▲Gloucester once had two stations – in the photograph my local hero 'Castle' Class 4-6-0 No. 5017 'The Gloucestershire Regiment 28th, 61st' leaves Central station c.1961 with an express for Paddington. My drawing depicts Eastgate station as it used to be before demolition – the northern end of the island platform was an ideal spot for trainspotting.

▼ On a trip to Carmarthen on 25 February 1963 I found my last 'Castle' needed to complete the class – lurking stored at the back of the shed was No. 4081 'Warwick Castle'. My lucky split pin (which I still carry with me) was taken from the running plate. The loco is seen in the photograph at Old Oak Common shed in 1962.

LOCOMOTIVES

on 28/29 March 1964 where 10 sheds were visited in the Glasgow and Edinburgh area in just one day. Although this was my first trip to Scotland it wasn't the last as I had met a likeminded lad from Gourock while trainspotting on Axminster station in August 1963 – for a year we corresponded with each other about our respective railway scenes and in August 1964 I spent a glorious week with Peter in Scotland – armed with a 'Freedom of Scotland' rail ticket we travelled far and wide, sallying forth each day from his home in Gourock, visiting 23 (mainly steam) engine sheds and travelling over many soon-to-be-closed lines on a railway system that was still very much dominated by steam. In September 1965 Peter visited me in Gloucester and we took this last opportunity to enjoy the steam swansong, travelling far and wide taking in the Somerset & Dorset, the Bulleid spectacular at Basingstoke and steam sheds at Bath, Oxford, Banbury, Birmingham, Derby, Nottingham, Colwick, Kirkby-in-Ashfield, Barrow Hill and Staveley. In 1966 I visited Peter again, this time capturing some of the last days of steam in Scotland – the highpoint was travelling on an Aberdeen to Buchanan Street express on 23 August hauled by 'A4' No. 60024 'Kingfisher' (I can still hear the chime whistle!).

▲ Candid camera – caught on film by my Scottish friend Peter Hughes (now residing in Vancouver) in a nonchalant pose at Basingstoke station on 10 September 1965 as 'West Country' Class 4-6-2 No. 34044 'Woolacombe' passes by. Peter disappeared out of my life in 1971 but, 40 years later, he contacted me from Vancouver after buying my *Lost Joy of Railways*.

By then I was nearly at the end of my trainspotting days – art college beckoned followed by years as a book designer in London. I did manage to get up to Bolton and Manchester in July 1968 to witness the end of steam but that was it! However, as you have probably noticed, it was not the end of the story – 40 years later my trainspotting days are still a vivid memory to me, thanks mainly to my late mother squirreling away my notebooks in her loft. I have much to thank her for as I would have probably thrown them away years ago – today, turning the thumbed pages still brings back very happy memories for me.

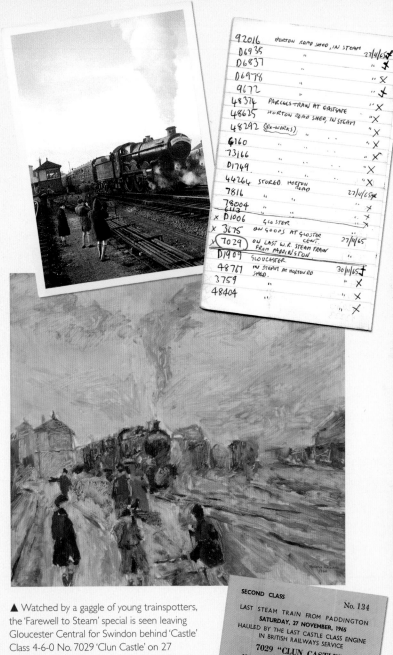

▲ Watched by a gaggle of young trainspotters, the 'Farewell to Steam' special is seen leaving Gloucester Central for Swindon behind 'Castle' Class 4-6-0 No. 7029 'Clun Castle' on 27 November 1965. This momentous event was also recorded for posterity in my notebook and in my painting executed at art college the following year.

Trainspotting

Collecting train numbers was a popular pursuit for young men before World War II, but the publication by Ian Allan of his first locospotters' guide in 1942 transformed the hobby.

Ian Allan (then an employee of the Southern Railway) published the *ABC of Southern Locomotives*, turning a minority interest into an all-consuming passion for thousands of men, young and old, across the country.

By the early 1950s a whole new publishing industry had grown up that documented every move of British Railways locomotives – magazines such as *Trains Illustrated*, *The Railway Magazine* and *Railway World* fed the craze along with a plethora of books such as Ian Allan's regional *ABC Locospotter* books, shed guides and directories.

By the 1960s steam haulage was doomed but the craze continued unabated, and there were still many diehard diesel enthusiasts out there who were prepared to stand on a draughty platform with their notebooks and cameras.

Sadly, the eradication of locomotive-hauled trains, the introduction of health and safety legislation and the fear of terrorism have all contributed to the downfall of this innocent and all-consuming passion. Those happy days are now but a fading memory for older people.

▲ Bereft of their nameplates but still looking well groomed, 'Royal Scot' 4-6-0s Nos. 46160 and 46152 attract the attention of trainspotters at Saltley shed on 15 September 1963 – the former loco was withdrawn from Kingmoor shed in May 1965. The latter loco masqueraded as No. 6100 on its visit to North America in 1933 and was withdrawn from Kingmoor in April 1965.

► The Ian Allan *ABC Combined Volume* was essential for any serious trainspotter. The 264-page Summer 1961 edition shown here not only listed all steam locomotives by region but had separate sections listing diesel locos and multiple units and electric locomotives and multiple units.

LOCOMOTIVES

◄ Published for 'boys of all ages' between 1916 and 1963, *Meccano Magazine* also included interesting features on Britain's railways.

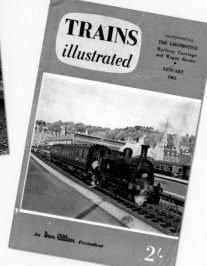

► Until 1962, *Trains Illustrated* featured articles on loco performance accompanied by good photo features. Loco shed reallocations were included as were growing lists of withdrawn steam locomotives.

▲ By 1966 steam locomotives still operating could be fitted into a 64-page guide. Ian Allan Locoshed Books were introduced twice a year detailing the shed allocation of each loco.

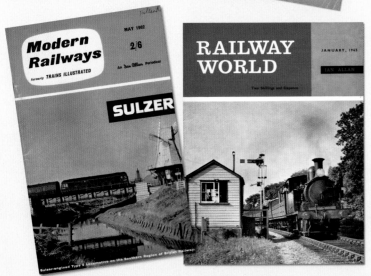

▲ In 1962 Ian Allan replaced the ever-popular *Trains Illustrated* monthly magazine with *Modern Railways*. In its early years the cover usually featured an advert by a company supplying railway equipment.

▲ Also published by Ian Allan, *Railway World* was a more learned monthly railway magazine which ceased publication in 2003. It was replaced by *Railways Illustrated*.

▲ Watching the trains go by – a group of trainspotters watch Stanier '8F' 2-8-0 No. 48318 head through Lichfield with a coal train on 13 April 1957.

All the Gear

Essential gear for a day out trainspotting included notebook, biro, locomotive shed directory, *ABC Combined Volume*, cheap camera, duffel bag and packed lunch. Optional extras could include a packet of five Woodbines!

Half-term February 25, 1963. Alarm goes off at 5.30am, hurriedly get dressed, have a quick bowl of cereal and a cup of tea and then, with duffel bag hitched over my shoulder, I was off on my Dawes racing bike down to Central station to catch the early morning train to Cardiff – local 'Hall' Class No. 4929 'Goytrey Hall' was at the head of our train. This was the first leg of a day's 'shed bashing' to Port Talbot Duffryn Yard (87B), Neath (87A), Llanelly (87F) and Carmarthen (87G). The object of the exercise was to cop the last 'Castle' needed to complete the underlining of this class in my Ian Allan *ABC of British Railways Locomotives Combined Volume*. Late that afternoon the object of my desires, No. 4081 'Warwick Castle', was found tucked away out of use behind Carmarthen shed. Mission accomplished!

The above story illustrates the dedication and, some would say, fanaticism that some trainspotters possessed to catch that last elusive number. Trainspotting books had been around before World War II but these were published by each of the Big Four railway companies. In 1942 a young Southern Railway clerk by the name of Ian Allan published his first book – the *ABC of Southern Locomotives*. Selling for the princely sum of one shilling, the book was an instant success and led to a whole series of regional

▲ Every trainspotter worth his salt had a small library of Ian Allan locomotive and shed guides. From early beginnings in 1942 when he published his first locospotters' guide, the *ABC of Southern Locomotives*, Ian Allan went on to build a small publishing empire catering for the trainspotting craze in the 1950s and 1960s. Essential titles were the *ABC Regional Guides*, the ABC Combined Volume, *Locoshed Book* and the *British Locomotive Shed Directory*.

◀ With only a small amount of pocket money and the earnings from a newspaper round it was quite a struggle to save up enough for even the cheapest camera. Cameras such as the Coronet and Brownie Box were favourite accessories for any trainspotter but, unless the sun was shining and the train was stationary, the results could often be dire!

▶ Prior to Ian Allan's publishing enterprise the 'Big Four' railway companies issued books with lists of their own locomotives 'specially arranged for engine spotters'. This LMS guide was published in 1947.

▶ Ian Allan's shed directory was an essential tool for locating engine sheds. This 1962 edition also provided itineraries for shed bashes around the country.

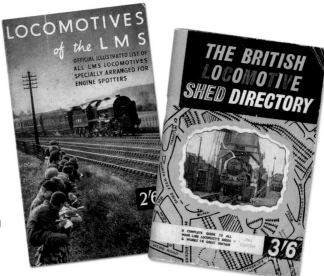

LOCOMOTIVES

► In the 1950s and 1960s special trains to railway works and locomotive sheds were organised for trainspotters by Ian Allan and various railway societies. Here 'A4' Class 4-6-2 No. 60014 'Silver Link' is at the head of a 1950s Ian Allan excursion.

ABC Guides, Loco Shed Books, Locolog Books and Locomotive Shed Directories, not to mention railway magazines such as *Trains Illustrated*. Trainspotting as a hobby had hit the big time. However, the *Combined Volume* (in 1962 costing 11/6) was every trainspotter's prize possession. Not only did it include lists (and photos) of every steam loco on British Railways by region but also, by that date, lists of the newly-introduced diesel and electric locos and even longer lists of those (then) unloved diesel and electric multiple units.

Of course, the *Combined Volume* wasn't the only item required for a day of trainspotting. Also packed in the duffel bag was the latest edition of Ian Allan's *Trains Illustrated* magazine, a notebook and pen for writing in the numbers of each loco spotted, a cheap camera (if you were lucky) like a Brownie Box or Coronet, a supply of Mum's wholemeal bread and Marmite sandwiches, an apple and a couple of cartons of Kia-Ora orange squash. Naturally, the neat underlining of loco numbers spotted was done back at home in the evening while listening to the latest Top 10 hit on Fabulous 208 Radio Luxembourg!

By February 25, 1963 the days were numbered for steam-haulage on passenger trains in South Wales. Apart from the solitary 'Hall' on the Gloucester to Cardiff stage, all of the other trains to Carmarthen and back on that day were hauled by 'Hymeks' or 'Westerns'.

◄ The result of a day's trainspotting in Hereford and Shrewsbury on April 18, 1964. The neat underlining was carried out after returning home.

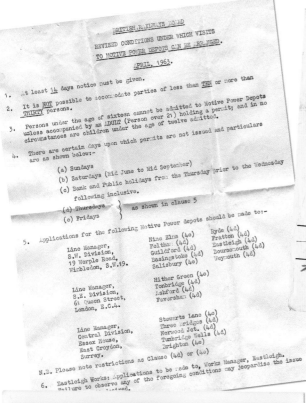

BRITISH RAILWAYS BOARD
REVISED CONDITIONS UNDER WHICH VISITS
TO MOTIVE POWER DEPOTS CAN BE ARRANGED.

APRIL, 1963.

1. At least 14 days notice must be given.

2. It is NOT possible to accommodate parties of less than TEN or more than THIRTY persons.

3. Persons under the age of sixteen cannot be admitted to Motive Power Depots unless accompanied by an ADULT (Person over 21) holding a permit; and in no circumstances are children under the age of twelve admitted.

4. There are certain days upon which permits are not issued and particulars are as shown below:-

(a) Sundays
(b) Saturdays (Mid June to Mid September)
(c) Bank and Public holidays from the Thursday prior to the Wednesday following inclusive.
(d) Thursdays } as shown in clause 5
(e) Fridays }

5. Applications for the following Motive Power depots should be made to:-

Line Manager,   Nine Elms (4e)   Hyde (4d)
S.W. Division,   Feltham (4d)   Fratton (4d)
19 Worple Road,   Guildford (4d)   Eastleigh (4d)
Wimbledon, S.W.19.   Basingstoke (4d)   Bournemouth (4d)
   Salisbury (4e)   Weymouth (4d)

Line Manager,   Hither Green (4e)
S.E. Division,   Tonbridge (4d)
61 Queen Street,   Ashford (4d)
London, E.C.4.   Faversham (4d)

   Stewarts Lane (4e)
Line Manager,   Three Bridges (4d)
Central Division,   Norwood Jct. (4d)
Essex House,   Tunbridge Wells (4d)
East Croydon,   Brighton (4e)
Surrey.

N.B. Please note restrictions as Clause (4d) or (4e).

6. Eastleigh Works: Applications to be made to, Works Manager, Eastleigh.
Failure to observe any of the foregoing conditions may jeopardise the issue
...

LONDON MIDLAND AND SCOTTISH RAILWAY COMPANY   E.R.O. 49086

DISTRICT GOODS & PASSENGER MANAGER'S OFFICE
Telephone:
Telegrams:
9/11, ST. STEPHENS ST.,
BRISTOL 1.

Your Reference

Our Reference PX2/1626   26 SEP 1947   19

Dear Sir,

In accordance with your request, I have been pleased to arrange for your visit to the undermentioned Motive Power Depot on the date and at the time shown.

On arrival at the Motive Power Depot, this permit should be presented immediately and a responsible member of the staff will conduct you round.

In the interests of safety, no person under 16 years of age will be allowed to visit a Motive Power Depot unless accompanied by an adult, and the visit will terminate before the hours of darkness. The only luggage permitted in the Motive Power Depot will be cameras, and photographs may be taken for private collection only.

Acceptance of this permission will constitute an agreement to relieve the Company of liability in the event of any personal injury or loss of or damage to property being sustained on the Company's premises.

I hope you have an instructive and enjoyable visit.

Yours faithfully,

for G. S. RIDER

Motive Power Depot to be visited	Date	Time	No. of Persons (Males only)
Bristol	5/10/47	2 pm	2

Mr. B. J. Ashworth
The Cottage
Gravel Hill
Wombourne
Nr. Wolverhampton.

◄ *(far left)* The ponderous rules issued by the Southern Region following an application for a shed pass in April 1963.

◄ *(left)* An LMS shed pass issued in September 1947 authorising a visit to Bristol Barrow Road shed.

▲ 'Well, I do know that this was the last Brit built!' – two young trainspotters are seen in a deep conversation about BR Standard 'Britannia' Class 4-6-2 No. 70054 'Dornoch Firth' at Preston in 1963.

Shed & Works Passes

During the 1950s and early '60s it was considered rather a 'cissy' thing to apply for a permit to visit an engine shed!

'Shed bashing', as it was known, was a term used by trainspotters to describe their frenetic trips to as many engine sheds (usually without permits) as was possible in one day.

Without an official permit, some sheds were easier to visit than others, depending on the friendliness of the shed foreman or the deviousness of the trainspotter. All manner of tricks were employed to gain access to the hallowed ground and once inside it was often a game of cat and mouse before we were eventually thrown out. However, many visits were official and highly organised by the myriad railway societies up and down the country, whose members were whisked from shed to shed by the coach load. It was a sad fact that many of these trips had to be made by road but (a) the trips were usually held on Sundays when the work force was at home digging the garden or out ferreting. The sheds were full and, because it was the Sabbath, there was only a limited or non-existent train service to the nearest station, and (b) there was no other practical way to visit such a large number of sheds as unfortunately many of them were located on out-of-the-way goods-only lines.

Naturally, the proper paperwork had been done by the Society and the necessary permits obtained. Annual open days at Crewe, Derby and Swindon for instance also drew large crowds of spotters. To accommodate the young spotter, Swindon Works

LOCOMOTIVES

also allowed visits without a permit on a Wednesday afternoon during the school holidays.

One memorable 'shed bash' that comes to mind was organised like a military campaign. On April 7, 1963 (a Sunday), the Warwickshire Railway Society took a coachload of members to nearly every shed in South Wales. Joining the coach on its way south in Gloucester at around 5.30am, we were soon traipsing round Lydney (85B sub-shed) before arriving at our next destination, Severn Tunnel Junction (86E) at 7am. During that long day we visited a total of 21 sheds and sub-sheds plus the Barry dump – Cardiff Cathays (88M) was also described in my notebook as a dump! In all we spotted 618 steam locos and only 43 diesels (mainly shunters). Despite the fact that we inexplicably didn't visit Abercynon (88E), it was an exhilarating and very profitable day. Just in time as well, as all of the steam sheds in South Wales had closed by 1965.

A very different 'shed bash' occurred a year later over the weekend of March 28/29, 1964. It may well have also been organised by the Warwickshire Railway Society, when a whole trainload of spotters departed from Birmingham New Street on the evening of the 28th behind No. 46256 'Sir William A. Stanier F.R.S.' – destination Glasgow! Arriving in Glasgow at the crack of dawn on the 29th, several hundred of us were bundled into a fleet of coaches which trundled from shed to shed until we reached Edinburgh Waverley later in the evening. Departure from Waverley was at 10.35pm with arrival at Birmingham New Street at 6am on the 30th. It was my first trip to Scotland and, by the end of the weekend, my notebook was filled to bursting with hundreds of 'foreign' locos. In all we visited ten sheds in the Glasgow and Edinburgh area and spotted a grand total of 349 steam locos and 312 diesels.

– 2 –

▲ *(top)* A prized lineside pass issued to railway photographer Ben Ashworth enabled him to record the final moments of steam in Gloucestershire.

▲ *(above)* A shed pass for Gloucester Horton road shed for a visit on September 26, 1965. Three months later the shed closed to steam. Of interest is the stipulation that any photographs taken were for private collection only.

◄ *(left)* The Stoke Division of the LMR issued detailed conditions for visits to their engine sheds, including the stipulation that visitors must travel by rail! No wonder so many trainspotters 'bunked' sheds without permission. Prior notification also had to be given if any females wished to travel with the party. Why?

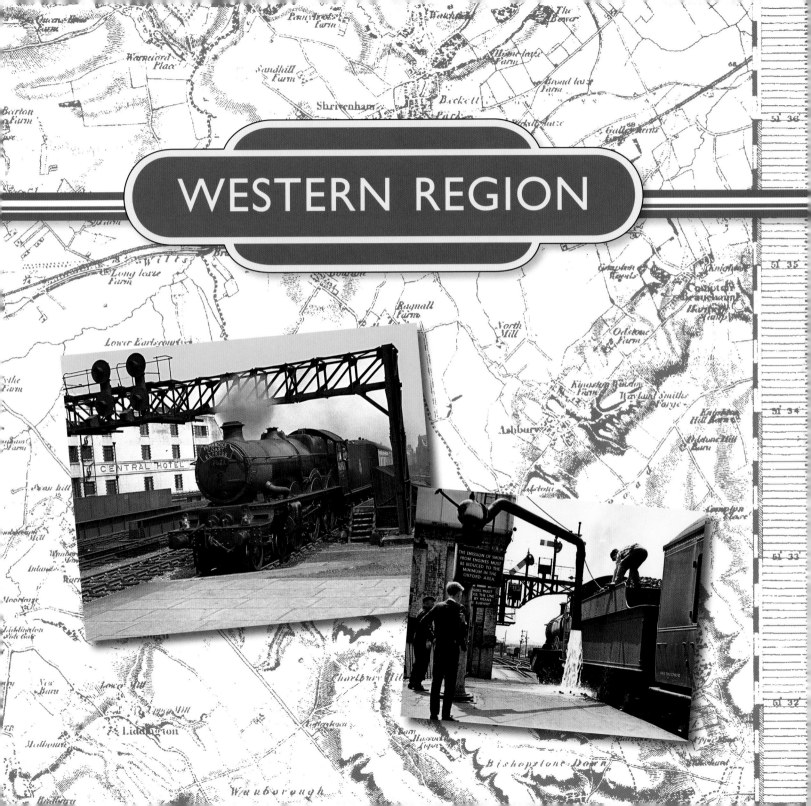

WESTERN REGION

London Paddington

The gateway to the West, Paddington station became the London terminus of the GWR in 1838. The present structure with its 14 platforms and graceful glazed roof and wrought iron pillars was designed by Isambard Kingdom Brunel and completed in 1854.

This busy station not only served the towns of the Thames Valley and Chilterns but was also the starting point for many of the famous named trains to the West. By the late 1950s the list of these steam-hauled trains was impressive and included the world-famous 'Cornish Riviera Express' to Penzance, 'The Mayflower' to Plymouth, 'The Merchant Venturer' to Weston-super-Mare, 'The Bristolian' non-stop to Bristol, 'The Capitals United Express' non-stop to Cardiff, 'The South Wales Pullman' to Cardiff, 'The Torbay Express' to Kingswear, 'The Pembroke Coast Express' to Pembroke Dock, 'The Inter-City' to Wolverhampton, 'The Red Dragon' to Carmarthen, 'The Cheltenham Spa Express' to Cheltenham Spa, 'The Royal Duchy' to Penzance, 'The Cambrian Coast Express' to Pwllheli and Aberystwyth and 'The Cathedrals Express' to Hereford.

At the same time Paddington was a Mecca for trainspotters with Old Oak Common shed providing top link 'Castles' and 'Kings' for the main line expresses and the more humble 6100 Class 2-6-2 tanks for suburban duties along with the unique Hawksworth-designed 1500 Class 0-6-0 tanks for empty coaching stock movements.

This period also saw for the first time the introduction of diesel-hydraulic locomotives on the main line expresses. Beginning with the five original North British A1A-A1A 'Warship' Class in 1958 diesel numbers started as a trickle but had ended as a flood by the early 1960s when the D800 B-B 'Warship' Class and the later D1000 C-C 'Western' Class took over many of the main line duties. By March 1965 the changeover was complete and Old Oak Common shed was closed to steam. Now, even those diesel loco-hauled trains are a distant memory with only the ageing HSTs providing a link back to those fascinating times.

◀ You can almost smell the oil, smoke and steam! Plenty of action at Paddington station around 4.45pm on 14 April 1962 – named trains seen were 'The Mayflower' (D830 'Majestic'), 'Cheltenham Spa Express' (No. 7035 'Ogmore Castle'), 'Cambrian Coast Express' (No. 6026 'King John'), Cathedrals Express' (No. 7007 'Great Western'), 'Cornish Riviera Express' (D 601 'Ark Royal') and the 'Red Dragon' (D7028).

◄ The date is March 24, 1951 and 'Castle' Class No. 4096 'Highclere Castle' stands at Platform 9 with the empty coaching stock of a train for Bristol Temple Meads. To the right, 'King' Class No. 6005 'King George II' is just arriving at Platform 10 with an express from Birmingham Snow Hill.

◄ The diesel-electric powered Blue Pullmans provided a 1st Class service between Paddington and Bristol, and Paddington and Wolverhampton Low Level. An additional service to Cardiff and Swansea was introduced in 1961. Following the transfer of Blue Pullmans from the LMR in 1967 additional services were introduced from Paddington to Bristol and Oxford. The service to Wolverhampton LL was withdrawn in 1967 and to Bristol and Swansea in May, 1973.

▲ A 'King' swansong – No. 6022 'King Edward III' gets ready to leave Paddington with an express for Birmingham on 9 September 1962. This handsome loco was withdrawn from Stafford Road shed later in the same month.

◄ Complete with train reporting number Z48 and Hawksworth tender, 'Castle' Class 4-6-0 No. 5054 'Earl of Ducie' at the head of an Oxford University Railway Society special at Paddington in May 1964. Less than 12 months later steam had disappeared from Paddington. No. 5054 was allocated to Worcester shed (85A) but was transferred to Gloucester in September 1964 and withdrawn.

Old Oak Common

81 A

▼ *A classic scene inside Old Oak Common shed in September 1955. Ex-GWR 'Star' Class 4-6-0 No. 4061 'Glastonbury Abbey', along with others of its class, was soon to be withdrawn. Only one, No. 4003 'Lode Star', has been preserved and can be seen in the National Railway Museum in York.*

The principal steam shed for the Western Region in London, Old Oak Common was opened by the GWR in 1906 on a site adjoining the Grand Union Canal just west of Paddington station. The nearest station was Willesden Junction (LMR and LTE) which was about ten minutes' walk away.

The largest engine shed on the GWR, it contained a total of four turntables, all of them under the cover of a pitched and glazed roof. Since closure to steam on March 22, 1965, part of it was retained as a stabling point for diesel locomotives and multiple unit trains.

A difficult shed to visit without a permit, Old Oak Common's October 1961 allocation of steam locomotives included 13 'King' Class 4-6-0s and 35 'Castle' Class 4-6-0s all kept in tip-top condition for hauling the principal expresses, such as the 'Cornish Riviera', 'Bristolian' and 'Red Dragon', and 11 'Halls', 14 'Modified Halls', 3 '4700' Class, 8 large 'Prairies' and a varied assortment of 49 0-6-0 tanks.

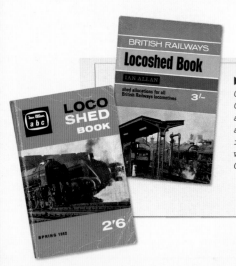

▶ *Double chimney 'Castle' Class 4-6-0 No. 5098 'Clifford Castle' shares the ash pit at Old Oak Common shed with a BR Standard '9F' 2-10-0 in 1962. This fine loco was withdrawn from Wolverhampton Oxley shed in June 1964.*

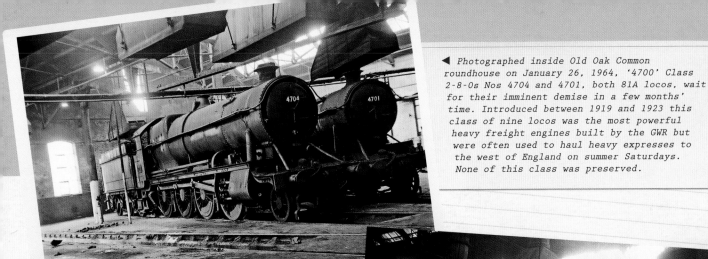

◀ Photographed inside Old Oak Common roundhouse on January 26, 1964, '4700' Class 2-8-0s Nos 4704 and 4701, both 81A locos, wait for their imminent demise in a few months' time. Introduced between 1919 and 1923 this class of nine locos was the most powerful heavy freight engines built by the GWR but were often used to haul heavy expresses to the west of England on summer Saturdays. None of this class was preserved.

▶ Ex-GWR 0-6-0 tanks wait for their next turn of duty inside Old Oak Common shed on May 11, 1963. On the left is '9400' Class No. 9495 which was built at Swindon after Nationalisation in 1949. In the centre is '9700' Class No. 9706 one of seven locos in this class which were introduced in 1933 and fitted with condensing apparatus for working through the tunnels of London Transport's Metropolitan Line.

◀ While Old Oak Common closed to steam in 1965 it continued life as a diesel stabling point. Seen here on 3 November 1973 are 'Western' Class diesel hydraulics (Class 52) Nos 1054 'Western Governor' and 1057 'Western Chieftain' and, nearest the camera, 'Hymek' (Class 35) diesel hydraulic No. 7022. Now that steam had disappeared the prefix 'D' had been painted out on two of the locos' numberplates.

Oxford

The city once possessed two stations: the GWR's General station, opened in 1852, and the LNWR's Rewley Road station, opened in 1851 and closed in 1951.

Oxford was unique on the Western Region as a focal point for trains from more than two regions (as witnessed at places such as Shrewsbury, Gloucester, Salisbury and Exeter). These inter-regional trains brought 'foreign' locomotives from the Southern Region via Basingstoke and Reading, the Eastern and Midland Regions via the former L&NWR route from Cambridge via Bletchley and the Eastern (subsequently Midland) Region from the former Great Central main line via Woodford Halse and Banbury. Consequently it was not uncommon to see the native former GWR locos rubbing shoulders with SR 'Battle of Britain' or 'West Country' Pacifics, ER Class B1s or even ex-LNWR 0-8-0 goods locos.

In addition to the regular appearance of these 'foreigners', the WR was well represented by 'Castles' on the 'Cathedrals Express' and other Paddington to Worcester and Hereford turns, 'Halls' and 'Granges' on mixed-traffic duties to Worcester, Banbury, Birmingham, Reading and Basingstoke, and the plain-Janes of heavy freight such as the 2800 Class 2-8-0s. Quite a heady mix which also included branch line trains from Fairford and Princes Risborough and has now disappeared forever.

▶ Ex-GWR 'Hall' Class 4-6-0 No. 6923 'Croxteth Hall' brings a down fitted freight into Oxford by Hinksey gasworks. No. 6923 was built at Swindon in 1941 and spent its last years allocated to Oxford shed (81F) before being withdrawn at the end of 1965. It was scrapped at Cashmore's, Newport, in May 1966.

◀ During the last month of steam on the Western Region, decrepit 'Modified Hall' 4-6-0 No. 6993 'Arthog Hall' (minus nameplates) passes through Oxford with an up coal train on 12 December 1965. No 6993 was built at Swindon in 1948 and finally ended up allocated to Oxford shed (81F) before being withdrawn less than three weeks after this photo was taken. The loco was scrapped at Cashmore's, Newport in 1966.

▲ Having just replaced a Southern Region loco, ex-LMS 'Jubilee' 4-6-0 No. 45581 'Bihar and Orissa' heads north out of Oxford station with a train from the south coast on 20 July 1963. Built by the North British Locomotive Company in 1934 and allocated to Farnley (55C) for many years, No. 45581 was withdrawn and scrapped in 1966. By contrast a fairly new diesel multiple unit can be seen approaching the station from the Banbury direction.

▶ Built at Swindon in 1950, 'Manor' Class 4-6-0 No. 7824 'Iford Manor' has just taken on water at Oxford before resuming its journey southwards with the 10.30 Birmingham Snow Hill to Hastings train on 20 July 1963. This summer-Saturdays train followed an interesting route southwards via Reading General, Guildford, Redhill, Brighton, Eastbourne, Bexhill Central and St Leonards (Warrior Square). No. 7824 was built at Swindon in 1950 and withdrawn in 1964.

ON SHED

Oxford

81 F

▼ *Oxford shed was often visited by 'foreign' locos from the Southern, Eastern and London Midland Regions. Here, in August 1954, ex-LNER Class 'D16/3' 4-4-0 No. 62585 has arrived on shed after working a passenger train over the cross-country route from Cambridge. Known as 'Claud Hamiltons' after the first loco of this type (D14 introduced by the Great Eastern in 1900), the last D16/3 in service, No. 62613, was withdrawn from March shed in 1960. Note the crew having their tea break and the ex-GWR AEC railcar, or 'Flying Banana, on the right of the picture.*

The ex-GWR shed at Oxford was located on the west side of the line north of the station and was about five minutes' walk via a footbridge over the Oxford Canal.

Originally opened in 1854 by the Oxford, Worcester & Wolverhampton Railway (later absorbed by the West Midland Railway and then the GWR in 1863), the shed was not only home to a varied selection of ex-GWR locos in the '50s and early '60s but was also regularly visited by 'foreigners' from other regions while hauling trains from and to the Southern, Midland and Eastern Regions.

In the 1950s and early '60s it would have been common to see SR Bulleid Light Pacifics, ex-L&NWR 7F 0-8-0s or ER 'B1' 4-6-0s rubbing shoulders with WR 'Halls' or 'Granges'. Oxford's allocation in October 1961 consisted of 9 'Halls', 5 'Modified Halls', 6 BR Standard Class 4 4-6-0s, 3 '1400' 0-4-2 push-pull tanks, 13 large 'Prairies', 2 '5101' Class 'Prairies' and 10 0-6-0 pannier tanks.

In January 1966 the shed became the last ex-GWR to close to steam. Oxford's only sub-shed Fairford was usually home to a Class 7400 or 5700 0-6-0 tank. For such a small shed it is unusual that it had a 55ft. turntable which was used to turn the tank locomotives so they did not run bunker first. The shed closed in June 1962 at the same time as the 25-mile branch line that it served.

◀ *A visitor from Nuneaton shed (2B) on October 28, 1961 is ex-LNWR Class G2a 7F 0-8-0 No. 49431 seen here 'cooking up' near the coaling stage. Known as 'Super Ds' the final four engines of this once numerous class were withdrawn at the end of 1964. No. 49395 has since been preserved.*

◄ Ex-GWR '2800' Class 2-8-0 No. 3855 looks rather the worse for wear at Oxford shed in March 1965. By this date, with only nine months to go before the end of steam on the Western Region, most locos were kept in a very sorry state with their brass name and number plates already removed away from temptation and the wandering hands and spanners of spotters!

◄ Despite the imminent end of steam on the Western Region, a visit to Oxford shed (left hand column) and Banbury shed (right hand columns) on September 7, 1965 recorded plenty of steam activity. The journey back from Banbury to Oxford on the York to Bournemouth train was behind 'Hall' Class 4-6-0 No. 4920 'Dumbleton Hall' - this loco has since been preserved.

▼ With just under four months to go before withdrawal, decrepit 'Grange' Class 4-6-0 No. 6848 'Toddington Grange' (minus name and numberplates) is coaled up at Oxford shed on September 9, 1965. Built at Swindon in October 1937 No. 6848 was cut-up at Cashmore's scrapyard, Newport, in 1966.

9789	44847	6951
6848	D1683	92013
4962	D310	44560
6956	6644	6916
9773	6911	48220
73003	6922	34051
7912	D3109	D1745
48490	6868	48603
6849	75005	46428
6861	6917	6976
6927	73066	(4920)
3775	6947	D1710
6998	6930	D1751
73031	6697	6903
D1709	92228	D1715
D5035	92067	D1603
D3967	48671	92074
D5002	73048	D7520
73014	6931	D1687
BANBURY 2D	6934	D6811

Birmingham Snow Hill

Opened by the GWR in 1852, Birmingham Snow Hill was one of two principal stations in the city (the other being New Street) and served that company's main line trains to London Paddington, Shrewsbury, Chester and West Wales.

I t was rebuilt and enlarged twice, firstly in 1871 with an overall glazed roof and, secondly, in 1912 with improved facilities. Sadly, with the diversion of all main line trains to New Street in 1967, Snow Hill's days were numbered and this grand building and adjoining Great Western Hotel were demolished in the 1970s. Since then a much smaller and modern station has been reopened on the site to serve cross-city trains and, more recently, through trains to London Marylebone.

Snow Hill was a great place for the trainspotter in the late 1950s and early 1960s. Highlights of each day included 'The Inter-City' express from and to Paddington (normally hauled by a 'King' Class 4-6-0), the dual-portion 'Cambrian Coast Express', normally 'King' or 'Castle'-hauled between Paddington and Shrewsbury, to and from Paddington and West Wales and 'The Cornishman', also 'Castle'-hauled between Wolverhampton Low Level and Bristol Temple Meads, to and from Wolverhampton LL and Penzance. In addition to other passenger services to Shrewsbury, Wrexham, Chester, Worcester via Stourbridge Junction and South Wales via Stratford-upon-Avon (often operated by twin AEC railcars Nos 33 and 38 plus corridor second complete with buffet facilities and then Swindon-built 'Cross-Country' diesel multiple units), Snow Hill also witnessed a succession of freight trains through its centre roads. The short-lived 'Blue Pullman' diesel multiple unit service to and from Paddington was also introduced in September 1960. It was very rare to see locos from other regions at Snow Hill apart from the odd football special which could bring 'foreigners' from both the Southern and Midland Regions.

▲ Watched by two trainspotters, 'Castle' Class 4-6-0 No. 5082 'Swordfish' heads the 'Cambrian Coast Express' at Snow Hill in 1959. Built at Swindon in 1939 this loco was originally named 'Powis Castle' but was renamed early in 1941 along with 10 other members of its class to commemorate World War II British aircraft. Allocated to Old Oak Common (81A) No 5082 was withdrawn in July 1962.

▼ Another group of spotters at the west end of Platform 8 watch 'Modified Hall' Class 4-6-0 No. 7908 'Henshall Hall' draw out parcels vans from Platform 10 on July 18, 1959. This loco was built at Swindon in early 1950 and was allocated to nearby Tyseley shed (84E, later 2A) for most of its life until withdrawal in October 1965.

▶ In ex-works condition local engine 'Grange' Class 4-6-0 No. 6861 'Crynant Grange' heads through Snow Hill with an up freight on May 11, 1961. This loco was built at Swindon in early 1939 and was withdrawn from Tyseley shed in October 1965.

▼ A busy scene on Platform 7 of Snow Hill station on August 18, 1962 as ex-GWR 'King' Class 4-6-0 No. 6002 'King William IV' arrives with the 6.30am train from Birkenhead to Paddington. Judging by the clock the train is only about a minute late and will, no doubt, leave punctually at 10am. Allocated to Wolverhampton Stafford Road (84A) No. 6002 was built at Swindon in 1927 and was withdrawn from service only a month after this photo was taken.

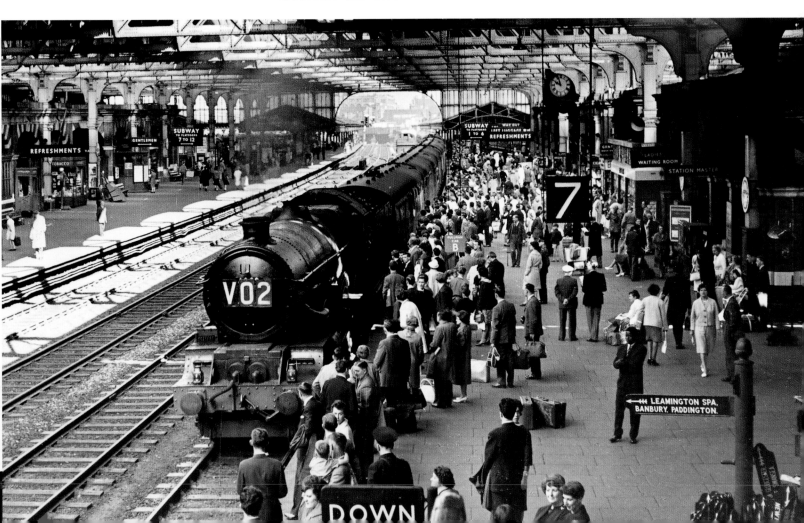

Worcester

85 A

▲ A busy scene at Worcester on February 17, 1962 with '8100' Class 2-6-2 tank No. 8107 and a '9400' Class 0-6-0 pannier tank being moved around the yard by a '5700' Class 0-6-0 pannier tank. On the left another '5700' Class 0-6-0 pannier tank receives some minor attention from the driver. With a total of ten locos the '8100' Class were rebuilds of the '5100' Class and were introduced in 1938. Two of them were allocated to 85A in 1962 but none of this class was preserved.

The ex-GWR shed at Worcester was located just north of Shrub Hill station in the triangle formed by the lines to Hereford and Droitwich. For the enthusiastic trainspotter it was just a 10 minute walk from Shrub Hill or quarter of an hour from Foregate Street station.

The shed, once also home to several of the ex-GWR AEC diesel railcars, consisted of two separate buildings totalling seven roads and in October 1961 had an allocation of 3 '2251' Class, 4 'Prairies', 3 '5600' Class, 6 Moguls, 6 'Halls', 5 'Modified Halls', 5 'Granges', 10 0-6-0 pannier tanks of various types, 2 BR Standard Class 4, 3 BR Standard Class 2 and last, but not least, 9 'Castles'. These were kept in tip-top condition for working 'The Cathedrals Express' and other main line services between Hereford, Worcester and Paddington. Included in this list were No. 7005 'Sir Edward Elgar' – named after the local composer – and No. 7007 'Great Western' – so named as it was the last steam engine built by the GWR before Nationalisation.

Even by 1962 the diesel-hydraulic invasion hadn't reached Worcester to any great extent and the Worcester-line trains remained some of the last to be steam-hauled out of Paddington. The shed was closed to steam at the end of 1965. Sub-sheds of Worcester were Evesham (closed 1961), Honeybourne (closed 1965), Kingham (closed 1962) and Ledbury (closed 1964).

▼ The ultimate in 'Castle' development - fitted with a double chimney and four row superheater No. 7004 'Eastnor Castle' was allocated to 85A when seen at the shed in February 1962. Built in 1946 this loco was withdrawn in January 1964. In addition to Nos. 7004 and 7005, Worcester was home to seven other 'Castles' - Nos. 7002, 7006, 7007, 7011, 7013, 7023 and 7027 - by the end of 1961.

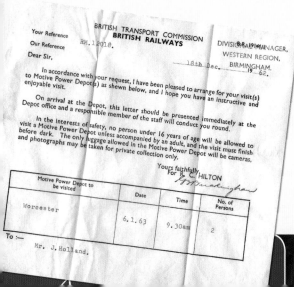

BRITISH TRANSPORT COMMISSION
BRITISH RAILWAYS

Your Reference
Our Reference RM.12018.

DIVISIONAL MANAGER,
WESTERN REGION,
BIRMINGHAM.
......18th Dec......19 62.

Dear Sir,

In accordance with your request, I have been pleased to arrange for your visit(s) to Motive Power Depot(s) as shewn below, and I hope you have an instructive and enjoyable visit.

On arrival at the Depot, this letter should be presented immediately at the Depot office and a responsible member of the staff will conduct you round.

In the interests of safety, no person under 16 years of age will be allowed to visit a Motive Power Depot unless accompanied by an adult, and the visit must finish before dark. The only luggage allowed in the Motive Power Depot will be cameras, and photographs may be taken for private collection only.

Yours faithfully,
For R. C. HILTON

Motive Power Depot to be visited	Date	Time	No. of Persons
Worcester	6.1.63	9.30am	2

To :-
Mr. J. Holland.

◀ This panoramic view of Worcester shed, circa 1962, clearly shows its triangular layout north of Shrub Hill station. Included in this view are several 'Castles' and 'Granges', a 'Manor', a '2251' Class 0-6-0 and a 'Black Five'. Worcester was the last WR shed to operate 'Castle' Class locos for regular main line express duties to Paddington.

▼ En route from Gloucester to Worcester shed on 15 December 1963 our trainspotter noted ex-LMS 'Princess' Class 4-6-2 No. 46201 'Princess Elizabeth' at Ashchurch. Withdrawn in 1962 this magnificent loco had been saved from the scrapyard and was initially kept at the Dowty Railway Preservation Society's site. On arrival at Worcester, 'Castles' No. 5054 'Earl of Ducie' and No. 7005 'Sir Edward Elgar' were at 85A along with a 'Grange' and a 'Jubilee'.

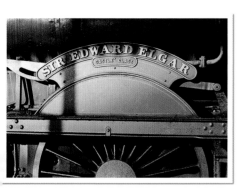

◀ Worcester was very proud of its nine 'Castles' and kept them in immaculate condition up until 1964. Star among them was No. 7005 'Sir Edward Elgar' which could regularly be seen in action on the 'Cathedrals Express' to Paddington. Built at Swindon in 1946 and originally named 'Lamphey Castle', No. 7005 spent its working life at Worcester until withdrawal in September 1964.

▶ With still very few diesels in evidence, our trainspotter noted a further five 'Castles' on his visit to 85A on December 15, 1963 – No. 5022 'Wigmore Castle', No. 7000 'Viscount Portal', No. 7023 'Penrice Castle', No. 7025 'Sudeley Castle' and No. 7031 'Cromwell's Castle'. Three of these, Nos. 5022, 7000 and 7031 had already been withdrawn from service.

Located to the West of Swindon station in the fork between the Swindon to Gloucester and Swindon to Bristol main lines, Swindon Works was the principal locomotive, carriage and wagon works for the Great Western Railway and, from 1948, the Western Region of British Railways.

OPENED IN 1841, THE WORKS transformed what was then just a rural village to a large railway town. Under the GWR's famous locomotive superintendents – Daniel Gooch, Joseph Armstrong, William Dean, G. J. Churchward, C. B. Collett and F. W. Hawksworth – the Works turned out firstly such broad gauge giants as the single-wheeler 2-2-2 and 4-2-2 express locos followed by the famous standard gauge 'City' and 'County' Class 4-4-0s, 'Star', 'Castle' and 'King' Class 4-6-0s and, at its peak in the 1930s, employed around 14,000 people.

Following nationalisation in 1948 Swindon turned its hand to building many of the BR Standard Class locos including 45 Class 3 2-6-2 tanks (Nos 82000-82044), 80 Class 4 4-6-0s, 20 Class 3 2-6-0 (Nos 77000-77019) and 53 Class 9F 2-10-0 including the last steam loco to be built for BR, No. 92220 'Evening Star'. The ill-thought-out Modernisation Plan of 1955 brought more work for Swindon including the building of 38 of the 'Warship' Class diesel-hydraulics (Class 42 D800-D832 and D866-D870) between 1958 and 1961, 35 'Western' Class diesel-hydraulics (Class 52 D1000-D1034) between 1961 and 1964 and 56 of the short-lived Type 1 diesel-hydraulics (Class 14 D9500-D9555) between 1964 and 1965 along with some of the more successful Class 03 0-6-0 diesel shunters and diesel multiple units – including some of the Inter-City, Cross-Country and trans-Pennine units. The last main line diesel locomotive to be broken up at Swindon was BR Sulzer Type 2 No. 25157 in March 1987.

Swindon was always popular with trainspotters in the 1950s and 1960s and armed with a permit it was possible to have a comprehensive guided tour of the Works, scrap line and engine shed on a Sunday. A tour of the Works only was available without a permit on Wednesday afternoons in the school summer holidays. Sadly, while the scrapyard continued cutting up main line diesels for a while longer, the Works closed in 1986 and all that is left to remind us of its illustrious past is the STEAM Museum of the Great Western Railway with its resident exhibits No. 4073 'Caerphilly Castle' and No. 92220 'Evening Star' and the former Engineer's Office which is now the headquarters of English Heritage.

▲ *The last Great Western express passenger engine built at Swindon was 'Castle' Class 4-6-0 No. 7037 'Swindon' which was built in 1950 and fittingly named to commemorate the works of her birth. Here she stands alongside fellow class member No. 5094 'Tretower Castle' undergoing repair in Swindon's famous 'A' shop in the mid 1950s.*

◀ *A visit to Swindon Works on 26 May 1963 found two withdrawn 'Kings' (Nos. 6011 and 6018) awaiting their fate outside while, inside the Works, there was an interesting mix of diesel and steam receiving attention – Crewe-built D1035 'Western Yeoman' was rubbing shoulders with several 'Warships', 'Halls', 'Modified Halls' and 'Granges'. Happy days!*

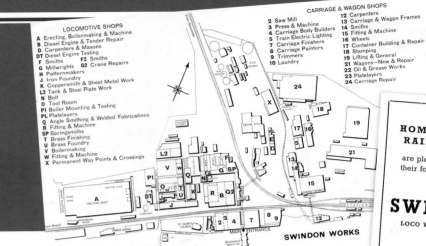

LOCOMOTIVE SHOPS
A Erecting, Boilermaking & Machine
B Diesel Engine & Tender Repair
C Carpenters & Masons
DT Diesel Engine Testing
F Smiths   F2 Smiths
G Millwrights   G2 Crane Repairs
H Patternmakers
J Iron Foundry
K Coppersmith & Sheet Metal Work
L2 Tank & Steel Plate Work
N Bolt
O Tool Room
P1 Boiler Mounting & Testing
PL Platelayers
Q Angle Smithing & Welded Fabrications
R Fitting & Machine
SP Springsmiths
T Brass Finishing
U Brass Foundry
V Boilermaking
W Fitting & Machine
X Permanent Way Points & Crossings

CARRIAGE & WAGON SHOPS
2 Saw Mill
3 Press & Machine
4 Carriage Body Builders
5 Train Electric Lighting
7 Carriage Finishers
8 Carriage Painters
9 Trimmers
10 Laundry
12 Carpenters
13 Carriage & Wagon Frames
14 Smiths
15 Fitting & Machine
16 Wheels
17 Container Building & Repair
18 Stamping
19 Lifting & General
21 Wagons—New & Repair
22 Oil & Grease Works
23 Platelayers
24 Carriage Repair

SWINDON WORKS

▲ Swindon Works built the entire class of 80 BR Standard Class 4 4-6-0s in the early 1950s. Here, on 27 September 1951, a near-complete loco is hoisted high in the main erecting shop to be paired up with its front bogies. Fondly remembered for their work on the Cambrian mainline in Wales during the last years of steam six members of this class have since been preserved.

► Swindon also built 53 of the BR Standard Class 9F 2-10-0 heavy freight locos. Here, No. 92213 is seen nearing completion in the main erecting shop in 1959. The last steam loco to be built at Swindon, also a 9F, and the last to be built by BR was the now-preserved No. 92220 'Evening Star' which was named in a ceremony at Swindon on March 18, 1960. Finished in gleaming BR Brunswick green and fitted with a copper-capped double chimney 'Evening Star' could be seen at work in the early 1960s hauling heavy passenger trains on the Somerset & Dorset Joint Railway from Bath Green Park to Bournemouth West and was later saved for preservation.

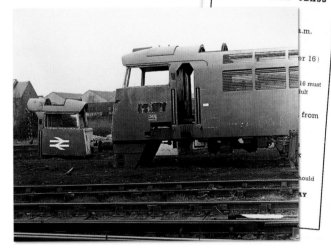

▲ Swindon built 35 of the 'Western' Class 52 diesel-hydraulics between 1961 and 1964. Although magnificent looking machines, the 'Westerns', along with the other types of diesel hydraulics, were plagued with unreliability and consequently had a very short life. Here, on 1 February 1975, the cab of No. 1007 'Western Talisman' and the body shell of No. 1019 'Western Challenger' end their days in the Swindon scrapyard.

Shrewsbury

Partially built over the River Severn, Shrewsbury's ornate station was opened in 1848 by the Shrewsbury & Chester Railway. With the opening of lines to Crewe and Birmingham the station soon came under the joint control of the GWR and the LNWR.

◀ Seen at Shrewsbury on April 18, 1964, ex-LMS 'Jubilee' Class 4-6-0 No. 45577 'Bengal', carrying the shed code 6D, waits to depart with a train for Swansea Victoria via the Central Wales Line. A year earlier Shrewsbury's shed code had changed from 89A to 6D following BR regional boundary changes.

Still an important junction, Shrewsbury was once a favourite haunt of trainspotters in the 1950s and 1960s. Numerous locomotive types from both the Midland and Western Regions rubbed shoulders here, with 'Royal Scots', 'Jubilees' and even 'Coronation' Pacifics being fairly common sights working through trains to the Midland Region via Crewe. LMR classes including 'Jubilees', 'Black Fives', Stanier 8F 2-8-0s and Fowler 2-6-4 tanks were also seen at work on trains to Swansea (Victoria) via the remote Central Wales Line – including the famous Swansea to York mail train. WR locomotive types ranged from 'Castles', 'Halls', 'Granges' and 'Counties' on trains to Birmingham, Chester and on the North-West route to Bristol and Cardiff via Hereford and the beautifully turned-out 'Manors' which hauled the 'Cambrian Coast Express' from Shrewsbury to Aberystwyth and Pwllheli. Despite being diesel-hauled from Paddington (usually by Brush Type 4s – later Class 47) from 1963, the last leg of this named train to West Wales continued to be steam-hauled up to 1967 – in their last season, these trains were hauled by BR Standard Class 4 4-6-0s and 2-6-0s. The continuous stream of north-south freight trains trundling through Shrewsbury station along with branch trains to Bridgnorth via the Severn Valley added to this rich tapestry.

▲ Ex-LMS Fowler 2-6-4T tank No. 42309 arrives at Shrewsbury with a train from Swansea via the Central Wales Line on May 6, 1960. This loco was built at Derby in 1928 and was withdrawn from Carnforth shed in September 1964.

◄ Shrewsbury was a trainspotter's paradise as witnessed here on June 11, 1963 when 'Coronation' Class Pacific No. 46251 'City of Nottingham' visited the station. The loco is seen here having just turned on the triangle around Severn Bridge Junction signal box. Allocated to Crewe North (5A) No. 46251 was repainted in BR red livery in November 1958 and carried this until withdrawal in October 1964.

▼ The last down steam-hauled 'Cambrian Coast Express' waits to leave Shrewsbury station for Aberystwyth behind unkempt double chimney BR Standard Class 4 4-6-0 No. 75006 on 11 February 1967.

▲ A trip from Gloucester to Shrewsbury on 18 April 1964 recorded plenty of steam and diesel activity. The journey from Gloucester to Hereford was behind 2-6-0 No. 6349 and from Hereford to Shrewsbury behind D861 'Vigilant'. Noted at Shrewsbury was 'Jubilee' Class 4-6-0 No. 45577 'Bengal' on a Central Wales Line train to Swansea Victoria, several 'Manors' on Cambrian Line duties and the Brush Type 4s which had already usurped steam on the Wolverhampton (LL) and Paddington trains.

Cardiff

Opened by the South Wales Railway in 1850, Cardiff General station was rebuilt in its present form by the GWR in 1932. it is The largest station in Wales.

Cardiff has always been an important railway hub with local trains to the Welsh Valleys and long distance services to Fishguard via Swansea and Carmarthen, Bristol, Portsmouth and London Paddington via the Severn Tunnel, the north via Newport, Hereford and Shrewsbury and the Midlands via Gloucester. Although still a very busy station, the scene during the 1950s and 1960s was very different.

Named expresses such as the 'Capitals United Express', 'The South Wales Pullman', 'The Pembroke Coast Express' and 'The Red Dragon' were in the charge of Cardiff Canton's 'Kings' or 'Castles' and for a few years at the end of the '50s also in the capable hands of the 12 'Britannias' that were also allocated to that shed. 'Halls', 'Modified Halls' and 'Granges' completed the line up on many of the other cross-country services and it was a daily occurrence to see SR malachite green livery coaches in Cardiff on the through service to Portsmouth Harbour via Bristol and Salisbury. Between the summer of 1961 and May 1973 the 'South Wales Pullman' to Paddington was operated by a Blue Pullman diesel train. Until the introduction of dmus in the early 60s many of the local Valley services were handled by 5600 Class 0-6-2 tanks. Goods traffic through Cardiff was exceptionally heavy with the long coal and iron ore trains in the charge of 2800 Class 2-8-0s, 4200 Class 2-8-0 tanks, 7200 Class 2-8-2 tanks, ex-WD Class 2-8-0s and the Standard 9F 2-10-0s.

The year 1962 was a turning point for Cardiff's band of trainspotters when Cardiff Canton steam shed was closed and all of its remaining allocation transferred to Cardiff East Dock shed (88L). A new diesel depot was opened at Canton and soon Cardiff General was humming with the sound of 'Western' and 'Hymek' diesel hydraulics, soon to be followed by Brush Type 4 and English Electric Type 3 diesels. Steam was finally ousted from the Cardiff area by the summer of 1965.

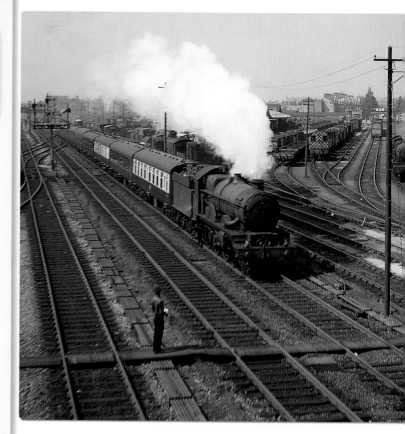

▲ With only six months to go before withdrawal, 'Castle' Class 4-6-0 No. 5043 'Earl of Mount Edgcumbe' passes Pengam Junction, Cardiff with an up express on June 30, 1963. This loco was built at Swindon in 1936 and originally named 'Barbury Castle'. Fitted with a double chimney and four row superheater in 1958 this loco ended its days at Cardiff East Dock shed. Fortunately No 5043 was sold to Dai Woodham in 1964 and subsequently saved for preservation by the Birmingham Railway Museum in 1973.

◀ 'King' Class 4-6-0 No. 6003 'King George IV' waits to back down to the up 'Red Dragon' express which has just arrived at Cardiff General from Swansea in September 1960.

▲ 'Castle' Class 4-6-0 No. 7027 'Thornbury Castle' enters Cardiff General at the head of the inaugural down 'Pembroke Coast Express' on Monday, June 8, 1953. Having left Paddington at 10.55am this train would reach its destination at Pembroke Dock at 5.26pm. No. 7027 was built at Swindon in 1949 and withdrawn in 1963. Fortunately it was bought by Dai Woodham in 1964 and has subsequently been saved for the preservation movement.

◀ The driver and fireman of 'Castle' Class 4-6-0 No. 5082 'Swordfish' wait patiently for Alan Jarvis to take his photo before they head off to Paddington with the up 'Pembroke Coast Express' on 8 August 1953. The express had only been introduced two months earlier and ran non-stop between Newport and Paddington with an average speed of more than a mile-a-minute.

The story of DAI WOODHAM's scrapyard at Barry in South Wales is well known but without him the majority of Britain's preserved steam locos would not be with us now.

▲ A sad scene at Woodham's scrapyard in Barry, South Wales following the end of steam on British Railways as an ex-LMS Black Five makes an impassioned plea.

▶ Some of the early arrivals at Dai Woodham's scrapyard at Barry. Here a long line of Western Region 0-6-0 pannier and 2-6-2 Prairie tanks make a sad sight in August 1961. Fortunately, of the 297 withdrawn steam locos bought by Woodham's between 1959 and 1968 only 80 were actually dismantled and scrapped. The rest is history!

IT ALL STARTED IN 1959 when Woodham's took their first delivery of Western Region withdrawn steam locos from Swindon – four 5300 Class Moguls and one 3100 'Prairie' tank. In these early days the scrapyard could keep pace with deliveries but as time went on the numbers steadily increased, not only from the Western Region but also, by 1964, from the Southern and London Midland Regions. In total, between 1959 and 1968, Woodham's bought 297 steam locos but scrapped less than a third.

The answer for this reprieve was simple – Woodham's had also bought vast amounts of redundant goods wagons and brake vans from BR and these were easier to dispose of than steam locos. These could wait until later but by then the growing railway preservation movement had other ideas and soon these rusting hulks were being carted off for their rebirth on preserved lines throughout the UK. Britain's railway enthusiasts have much to thank Dai Woodham for as he inadvertently saved 213 steam locos. Many of them lay rusting at Barry for over 20 years with the longest resident being ex-GWR 2-6-2 tank No. 5552 which arrived in May 1961 and was liberated in June 1986 – more than 25 years on 'death row'.

Western Region locos saved include 11 'Hall', five 'Castle', two 'King', six 'Modified Hall' and eight 'Manor' 4-6-0s. Representatives of the Southern Region, particularly Bulleid Pacifics, fared even better as most of them were withdrawn towards the end of steam on BR and include 10 'West Country', eight 'Battle of Britain' and 10 'Merchant Navy' Pacifics. Even two Somerset & Dorset Joint Railway 7F 2-8-0s and the unique BR 8P Pacific No. 71000 'Duke of Gloucester' were fortunately saved for posterity.

The Miracle of Barry Scrapyard

▼ Although Woodham's bought a total of 28 SR Bulleid Pacifics only two, Nos. 34045 and 34094 were actually scrapped. Here, unrebuilt 'West Country' No. 34094 'Mortehoe' is seen being cut up on January 10, 1965.

▲ Thousands of locomotives passed into private scrapyards during the 1960s and most disappeared within months, but despite Woodham's receiving some 297 engines, few were scrapped and this 'stay of execution' enabled preservationists to build up funds and save types which would otherwise have become extinct. The centrepiece in this view of Woodham's sidings is SR 'U' Class 2-6-0 No. 31625 which arrived in June, 1964. She lay in the scrapyard for 16 years, until purchased for preservation in 1980.

▼ Woodham's bought 35 ex-LMS steam locos between 1964 and 1968. Of these only two, Ivatt 2-6-2 tanks Nos. 41248 and 41303, were cut up. The rest were saved for preservation including 'Jubilee' Class 4-6-0 No. 45690 'Leander' seen here at Barry on April 24, 1965. This now-famous loco, one of only four of its class to be preserved, was withdrawn from Bristol Barrow Road (82E) in March 1964, arrived at Woodham's in July and left for preservation in May 1972.

▶ A visit to Woodham's on April 7, 1963 found 31 condemned steam locos, all WR types. The stars of the show were the 'King' Class 4-6-0 Nos 6023 'King Edward II' and 6024 'King Edward I'. They had arrived at Barry late in 1962. No. 6023 spent 22 years at the yard before being saved for preservation in 1984. No. 6024 was saved in March 1973, after 10 years on 'death row'.

Cardiff Canton

88 A

▲ *Ex-GWR '4575' Class 2-6-2 tanks Nos. 5572 and 4578 at the end of the fire-dropping and coaling queue at Canton shed on September 6, 1953. Fourteen of these locos were saved for preservation, of which 13 were rescued from the nearby Barry scrapyard.*

Located just to the west of Cardiff General station and originally opened by the GWR in 1882 and considerably extended by them in 1925 and 1931, Canton shed was the principal main line steam shed in Cardiff and was given the code 86C until 1960. It was about 10 minutes walking time from General station.

Along with the regular 'Kings' and 'Castles' allocated for top link jobs on expresses to Paddington, Canton was also allocated 12 'Britannia' Class 4-6-2s for a short while in the late 50s and early 60s until they were reallocated to Carlisle Kingmoor (12A) and Aston (21D). In October 1961 Canton's impressive allocation included 7 '2800' Class 2-8-0s, 5 '4200' Class 2-8-0 tanks, 3 Moguls, 19 0-6-0 pannier tanks of various types, 2 'Manors', 5 'Granges', 3 'Modified Halls', 21 'Halls', 15 'Castles', 3 'Kings', 7 ex-WD 2-8-0s and 11 BR Standard 9F 2-10-0s including No. 92220 'Evening Star' – the last steam locomotive to be built by BR.

After closure to steam in September 1962 a new diesel depot was opened on the site and all of Canton's remaining steam locomotives were reallocated to Cardiff East Dock (88L). The new diesel depot serviced 'Hymek' and 'Western' diesel-hydraulics and the English Electric Type 3 (later Class 37) and Brush Type 4 (later Class 47) diesels for many years.

▼ *Ex-GWR '2800' Class 2-8-0 No. 2876 pollutes Cardiff's skies at Canton in March 1961. This heavy freight loco was built at Swindon in 1919 and spent the majority of its life allocated to various South Wales sheds before being withdrawn from Newport Ebbw Junction shed in early 1965. Preservation groups have saved 16 of these fine locos, of which 15 were rescued from the famous Barry scrapyard.*

◀ *Ex-Alexandra (Newport and South Wales) Docks & Railway Company 2-6-2 tank No. 1205 is seen here a year after withdrawal at Canton shed on 18 July 1957. The A. D. & R. Company and its 39 locos, including No. 1205, became part of the GWR in 1922 when the two companies were merged.*

Cardiff East Dock

88 L

◄ The filthy task of cleaning the smokebox of a Stanier '8F' 2-8-0 at Cardiff East Dock shed in March 1963. Despite our nostalgia for steam the cleaners must have jumped for joy when diesels were introduced.

Located in Cardiff's Docklands, Cardiff East Dock shed was a 30 minute walk for the trainspotter from General station past Bute Docks and Roath Basin.

Built by the GWR in 1931, the shed was originally coded 88B until 1958 and provided steam motive power for the extensive rail network around Cardiff's Docks. It later became a diesel depot (code CED) with an allocation in October 1961 of 40 of the standard BR 0-6-0 shunter and the entire class of 1948 Swindon-built 0-6-0 shunters numbered 15101 to 15106. Destined for early closure, Cardiff East Dock's fortunes revived in September 1962 when it received the remaining steam locos displaced by the closure of Canton shed.

Until closure in August 1965 it was common to see a motley collection of decrepit ex-GWR main line steam locos around the shed – for instance on Sunday April 7, 1963 there were 44 steam locos (all ex-GWR except for one Stanier 8F 2-8-0) including 2 'Counties', 2 'Granges', 6 'Halls', 2 'Modified Halls' and 7 'Castles'.

▲ A 'foreign' visitor seen at Cardiff East Dock in July 1964 was SR 'U' Class 2-6-0 No. 31613 which was making its own way to Cohen's breaker's yard at Morriston in Swansea. On the right is 'County' Class 4-6-0 No. 1010 'County of Caernarvon' which was also withdrawn that month after only 18 years' service from Swindon shed (82C).

▼ Heavy freight workhorses of BR line up outside Cardiff East Dock on July 6, 1965 - less than a month before closure of the shed. Two Standard Class '9F' 2-10-0s, including 92166, and Stanier '8F' 2-8-0 No. 48636 await their next turn of duty. Then allocated to Birkenhead (6C) the '9F' was finally withdrawn in November 1967.

◄ Four of the seven 'Castles' found at Cardiff East Dock (88L) during a Warwickshire Railway Society 'shed bash' to South Wales on April 7, 1963.

◄ The three other 'Castles' seen on that trip in 1963. Note also the presence of two 'County' Class 4-6-0s and the trainspotter's comment about Cathays shed (88M)!

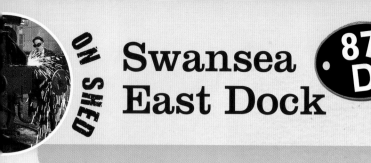

ON SHED

Swansea East Dock

Swansea East Dock was a good 20 minute walk from Swansea High Street station or, alternatively, a ride on a United Welsh bus heading towards Neath.

The shed was opened by the GWR in 1893 and provided locos for the extensive rail network serving Swansea Docks and associated heavy freight trains. The shed's allocation of 48 locos in October 1961 were all tank engines and included 28 0-6-0 pannier tanks of various types, 4 '4200' 2-8-0 tanks, 3 '7200' 2-8-2 tanks, and '5600' 0-6-2 tanks. To traverse the sharp curves around the docks the shed was also home to the two ex-Powlesland & Mason 0-4-0 saddle tanks Nos 1151 (built 1916) and 1152 (built 1912) and ex-Cardiff Railway 0-4-0 saddle tank No. 1338 dating from 1898. No. 1152 was soon withdrawn and the shed was allocated two unusual 'foreigners' in the shape of ex-LMS 0-4-0 saddle tank No. 47003 and ex-Lancashire & Yorkshire Railway 0-4-0 saddle tank No. 51218 of 1901 vintage.

Set in a bleak, windswept landscape Swansea East Dock finally closed in June 1964. Sub-sheds of Swansea East Dock were Gurnos (closed 1962) and Upper Bank (closed 1963).

▲ Far from its home territory in northern England veteran 0F 0-4-0 saddle tank No. 51218 stands forlornly out of use at Swansea East Dock in October 1963. Designed by John Aspinall for the Lancashire & Yorkshire Railway and introduced in 1901, this loco's short wheel base enabled it to traverse the sharp curves that abounded around Swansea Dock's rail system. Previously allocated to Bristol Barrow Road (82E) before moving to Swansea, No. 51218 was fortunately preserved and can now be seen on the Keighley & Worth Valley Railway.

▼ Another, more modern, 'foreigner' allocated to Swansea East Dock in October 1963 was ex-LMS 0-4-0 saddle tank No. 47003. Built by Kitson & Co of Leeds for the LMS the first five members of this class were introduced in 1932. A further batch of five locos with extended side tanks and increased coal space were built at Horwich by British Railways in 1953. Formerly allocated to Hasland shed (18C), No. 47003 and the other nine members of this class had all been withdrawn by 1966. Sadly, none was preserved.

◄ With only eight months to go before closure Swansea East Dock shed was a rather sad place to visit in October 1963. Fortunately, the four short-wheel base 0-4-0 saddle tanks were still there, although three of them were stored out of use by then.

▼ *The bleak line-up of stored locos at Swansea East Dock on October 27, 1963 - from left to right former Powlesland & Mason 0-4-0 saddle tank No. 1151, ex-Cardiff Railway 0-4-0 saddle tank No. 1338, 2-8-0 tank No. 4264, 0-6-0 pannier tanks Nos. 3781 and 6724 and 2-8-0 tank No. 5237.*

▲ *Another Kitson-built loco to be seen at Swansea East Dock was 0-4-0 saddle tank No. 1338. Here, seen out of use in October 1963, the loco was built in 1898 for the Cardiff Railway and spent its life on shunting duties around the docks of South Wales. Fortunately, this diminutive loco has since been preserved and can be seen at the Didcot Railway Centre.*

▶ *Although of a standard GWR design originally introduced in 1929, 5700 Class 0-6-0 pannier tank No. 6777, seen here at Swansea East Dock shed in October 1963, was one of only 15 members of this class built in 1950 after Nationalisation. The standard GWR shunting loco, a total of 863 were built of which 16 have been preserved.*

Gloucester

Once served by both the GWR and Midland Railway, Gloucester featured in the famous 19th century break-of-gauge cartoon when it was an important transhipment centre between Brunel's broad gauge and the standard gauge of the Midland Railway.

For the young trainspotter in the late 1950s and early '60s Gloucester couldn't fail to impress. With two engine sheds and two through stations it was here that a wide range of ex-GWR and ex-LMS locos could be seen at work. On the ex-GWR side was Central station and Horton Road shed. From here the top-link working was the 'Cheltenham Spa Express' and other unnamed trains to Paddington via Swindon always hauled by a gleaming 85B 'Castle'. Trains to Newport and Cardiff were usually in the capable hands of 'Halls' while the single-track route to Hereford saw a varied selection ranging from Class 4300 Moguls to 5101 Class 2-6-2 tanks. Interspersed were the 1400 Class 0-4-2 tanks on the Chalford auto trains and either 9400 Class 0-6-0 or 5101 Class 2-6-2 tanks on the short run to Cheltenham St James and ex-GWR AEC railcars on the Ledbury branch. Heavy freight to and from South Wales and the Midlands was usually in the capable hands of Class 2800 2-8-0s and Class 7200 2-8-2 tanks and the continuous stream of iron-ore trains from Banbury to South Wales were usually headed by BR Standard 9F 2-10-0s or ex-WD 2-8-0s. By 1965 nearly all main line operations were in the hands of the 'Warship', 'Western' and 'Hymek' diesel-hydraulics, Brush Type 4 and English Electric Type 3 diesels. Gloucester Eastgate station (linked to Central station by a very long footbridge) and Barnwood shed served the distinctly separate ex-MR route from Birmingham to Bristol. Here 'Black Fives', 'Jubilees', unrebuilt 'Patriots', Standard Class 5s and Class 2P 4-4-0s and 4F 0-6-0 goods engines were the order of the day until overtaken by the 'Peak' diesel invasion of the early 60s. Highlights of each day were

◀ With Gloucester Cathedral in the distance and viewed from the long overbridge linking Eastgate and Central stations ex-LMS 'Jubilee' Class 4-6-0 No. 45668 'Madden' manoeuvres a train out of the carriage sidings at Gloucester, c.1960. Built at Crewe in 1935, 'Madden' ended its days at Burton shed (17B) before being withdrawn at the end of 1963.

▲ Sheffield Millhouses (41C) engines were a fairly common sight at Gloucester working trains down to Bristol. Here, ex-LMS 'Royal Scot' Class 4-6-0 No. 46164 'The Artists' Rifleman' (in a fairly decrepit condition and minus nameplates) departs from Gloucester Eastgate with a summer-Saturday train for the north in September 1962. This loco was built at Derby in 1930 and was withdrawn soon after this photo was taken.

named trains such as the 'Pines Express' and 'Devonian' – usually 'Jubilee' or 'Black Five'-hauled – and 'The Cornishman' – always hauled by an immaculate Wolverhampton Stafford Road (84A) 'Castle'. The Docks branch, usually worked by diminutive ex-MR Deeley 0-4-0 tanks, also saw brand new London Underground stock, BR diesel railcars and coaching stock for far-flung parts of the British Empire such as Sierra Leone and Nigeria emerging like new full-size toys from the Gloucester Railway Carriage & Wagon Works.

The twilight of steam in Gloucester during 1963 and 1964 also saw the introduction of filthy and run-down 'Britannias' and 'Royal Scots' on the summer-Saturday trains from the Midlands and the North to the south west via Bristol. All local stopping and branch trains were withdrawn in late 1964 and steam had virtually disappeared by the end of 1965. Gloucester Eastgate clung to life but it was closed at the end of 1975 and then demolished.

▲ 'Hall' Class 4-6-0 No. 4929 'Goytrey Hall' passes its homes shed at Horton Road as it heads an FA Cup Final special to Wembley in 1961. The loco spent its last six years allocated to 85B until withdrawal in March 1965.

▼ Watched by a crowd of trainspotters, preserved 'Castle' Class 4-6-0 No. 4079 'Pendennis Castle' has just arrived at Gloucester Central with an LCGB special on 20 November 1965.

► This notebook page records activity at Gloucester Horton Road during the last two weeks of steam in December 1965 – the last surviving 'Castle' Class, No. 7029 'Clun Castle', eking out its last days on menial duties and Brush Type 4 D1901 hauling the last train to and from Cheltenham St James on 1 January 1966.

Gloucester Horton Road

85 B

Built by the GWR in 1854 and subsequently enlarged in 1921 this 6-road shed still possessed 35 steam locomotives as late as 1965. Walking time from Central station was about 10 minutes. Entry to the shed, through a hole in the fence, was not difficult for trainspotters!

In October 1961 Gloucester's allocation included 4 of the '1400' Class 0-4-2 tanks for the Chalford auto trains, 6 '2251' Class, 13 'Prairies' mainly for use on the Cheltenham St James run, 7 Moguls, 2 '5600' Class, 19 0-6-0 pannier tanks of various types, 5 'Halls', 3 'Modified Halls' and 8 'Castle' Class 4-6-0s which were used mainly on the Cheltenham Spa to Paddington expresses including the 'Cheltenham Spa Express', a descendant of the pre-war 'Cheltenham Flyer'. Possessing one of the largest nameplates of any steam locomotive on BR, a regular on this run was No. 5017 'The Gloucestershire Regiment 28th, 61st' – originally 'St Donats Castle' and renamed in 1954 after that regiment's heroic stand at the Battle of the Imjin River during the Korean War. Horton Road closed to steam on the first day of 1966.

Sub-sheds of Horton Road were Brimscombe (closed 1963), Cheltenham Malvern Road (closed 1963), Lydney (closed 1964) and Ross-on-Wye (closed 1963). Brimscombe shed usually housed a 'Prairie' tank which was kept there for banking heavy freight trains up Sapperton Bank. Lydney and Ross-on-Wye supplied locos for duties on the network of lines in the Forest of Dean.

▲ *Happier days at Horton Road. Ex-GWR '1400' Class 0-4-2 tank tops up with water prior to working an auto train to Chalford and back on May 15, 1964. In the background are '4300' Class 2-6-0 No. 6349 and '4500' Class 2-6-2 tank No. 4564. The Chalford auto train, the delightfully rural line to Hereford and all local stopping train services were all withdrawn by the end of that year.*

◄ *After the nearby ex-LMS shed at Barnwood (85C) had closed in 1964 visiting LMR locos were serviced at Horton Road. Here, with an admiring young audience, ex-LMS 8F 2-8-0 No. 48395 lies silent between a BR Sulzer Type 4 and Brush Type 4 D1642.*

▼ *By July 1963 the diesel-hydraulic invasion had reached Horton Road. Here, only four months old, 'Western' Class D1056 'Western Sultan' rubs shoulders with two 85B regulars - 'Modified Hall' 4-6-0 No. 6993, 'Arthog Hall' and 'Hall' Class 4-6-0 No. 5951, 'Clyffe Hall'.*

Gloucester Barnwood

85 C

▲ *Two ex-Midland Railway Deeley 0-4-0 tanks were allocated to Barnwood shed for working the maze of lines around Gloucester Docks. In September 1962 both No. 41537 and No. 41535 could be seen at rest in the shed. Access to the docks and to the Gloucester Railway Carriage & Wagon Company's works was via an ungated crossing over Parkend Road adjacent to California Crossing on the ex-Midland route towards Bristol.*

A typical Midland Railway roundhouse, Barnwood shed was opened in 1890 and closed in May 1964. For the trainspotter walking time from Eastgate station was about 15 minutes and access was fairly easy along a cinder path from Tramway Crossing. Engines awaiting the cutter's torch were usually stored on a long siding to the west of the shed. Barnwood's allocation provided motive power in the form of ex-MR, ex-LMS and BR Standard types for local passenger services to Bristol and Worcester, the Dursley, Nailsworth and Tewkesbury branches and local trip workings to Bristol Road gasworks and Gloucester Docks. The shed's allocation in October 1961 included the following 'maids of all work': 2 ex-MR Deeley 0-4-0 dock tanks, 5 ex-MR Johnson 3F 0-6-0s, 7 ex-LMS 4F 0-6-0s, 2 'Jinties' and 3 BR Standard Class 5 4-6-0s.

Sub-sheds of Barnwood were Dursley (closed 1962) and Tewkesbury (closed 1962).

◄ *Both allocated to Barnwood shed where they were photographed at rest on November 26, 1961. On the left is ex-MR Johnson 3F 0-6-0 No. 43645 which was a familiar sight pottering up and down the docks branch and on other local freight trains. On the right is ex-LMS Fowler 0-6-0 No. 44209 which travelled further afield and could occasionally be seen working local passenger trains to Bristol.*

▲ *A busy scene at Barnwood shed on a cold and sunny December morning in 1962. Getting up steam from left to right are 8F 2-8-0s Nos. 48420 and 48182 and 'Black Five' 4-6-0 No. 44819.*

Bristol Temple Meads

A historic station, the original part of Temple Meads was opened in 1840 as the western terminus of Brunel's GWR broad gauge route from Paddington.

▲ Fitted with double chimney and four row superheater, 'Castle' Class 4-6-0 No. 7018 'Drysllwyn Castle' of Bath Road shed (82A) gets ready to leave Temple Meads with the up non-stop 'Bristolian' to Paddington in the late 1950s. This particular train covered the 117.5-mile journey to London (via Badminton) in 102.5 minutes, arriving 2.5 minutes early at its destination. Occasionally completing this journey in under 94 minutes, the highly successful 'Castles' were replaced by 'Warship' diesel hydraulics in 1959.

More routes soon opened to the Midlands via Gloucester and the south west via Exeter and Plymouth leading to an expansion of the station, including the building of the overall glazed roof, in 1870. The GWR carried out further improvements to the station in the 1930s.

Bristol Temple Meads was pure joy for the trainspotter in the 50s and early 60s – with not only the continuous stream of passenger trains from north, south, east and west but also the comings and goings around the adjoining Bath Road engine shed. Services to and from the north and the Midlands were handled by Barrow Road's allocation of 'Jubilees', unrebuilt 'Patriots' and Standard Class 5s. Sightings of LMR locos from Saltley, Derby and Leeds Holbeck were also a common sight. It was at Temple Meads that named trains such as 'The Devonian' and 'The Cornishman' ('Castle'-hauled from Wolverhampton LL) had a change of engines. There were sleeping car services to Scotland and stopping trains to Gloucester, often in the charge of 2P 4-4-0s, and to Bath Green Park via Mangotsfield. Summer Saturdays saw a continuous stream of holiday trains from the north and Midlands to the holiday resorts of Devon and Cornwall – in the twilight of steam many hauled by filthy 'Britannias', 'Royal Scots' and 'Castles' and even the odd ER 'B1'.

The top link WR train was surely 'The Bristolian', but the last steam-hauled up service was hauled by 'Castle ' Class 4-6-0 No. 5085 'Evesham Abbey' on June 12, 1959. After that date it was 'Warships' and downhill! The 'Bristol Pullman' to Paddington was operated by Blue Pullman diesel sets between 1960 and 1973.

▼ 'Blood and custard' heads south for the holidays! On a sunny summer Saturday in early BR days an ex-LMS Stanier 'Black Five' 4-6-0 departs from Temple Meads with a Birmingham to Paignton express. The station's overall roof was added during enlargements in 1870. Despite the disappearance of steam and some track rationalisation the scene remains little changed today.

A group of trainspotters admire Old Oak Common's gleaming 'Castle' Class 4-6-0 No. 5035 'Coity Castle' at Bristol Temple Meads in 1959.

Temple Meads was also busy with services to Exeter and Plymouth and cross-country services to Cardiff, Westbury and Portsmouth. Local services to Portishead, Severn Beach and Frome via Radsotck added to the hustle and bustle. Bath Road closed to steam in September 1960 and a new diesel depot was built on the site to cater for the ever-increasing numbers of 'Warships', 'Westerns' and 'Hymeks' with the remaining steam locos moving to St Philip's Marsh shed. The latter closed in June 1964 and the remaining steam servicing was carried out at Barrow Road until November 1965 when that, too, was closed.

▲ Opened in 1840 as the terminus of Brunel's broad gauge line from Paddington, the western part of Temple Meads station was usually the starting point for trains on the former Midland route to Gloucester and Birmingham. Here ex-LMS 'Black Five' 4-6-0 No. 44825 of Saltley shed (21A) blows off steam before drawing forward with a stopping train for Gloucester on 7 September 1963. All stopping train services on this route were withdrawn in January 1965.

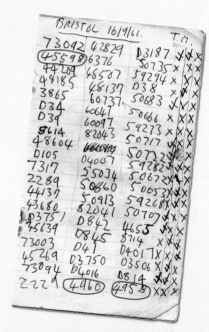

▲ A trip to Bristol Temple Meads on 16 September 1961 recorded plenty of steam and diesel activity – notable among the former were 'Jubilee' Class 4-6-0 No. 45598 'Basutoland' and 'Hall' Class 4-6-0s No. 4960 'Pyle Hall' and No. 4958 'Priory Hall'. Completing this fascinating scene were plenty of dmus, 'Peak' and 'Warship' diesels.

ON SHED

Bristol Bath Road

82 A

▼ *A general view of Bath Road shed taken towards the end of the steam era, c.1959. At its peak as a steam shed Bath Road had an allocation of around 20 'Castles' of which two, both 82A locos, can be seen here. On the left is No. 5090 'Neath Abbey' which was rebuilt from 'Star' Class 4-6-0 No. 4070 (also named 'Neath Abbey') in 1939. It was withdrawn in 1962. On the right, with train reporting number M96, is No. 5078 'Beaufort' which was built in 1939 and originally named 'Lamphey Castle'. Later fitted with a double chimney and four row superheater this loco was also withdrawn in 1962.*

Replacing an earlier shed originally opened by the Bristol & Exeter Railway in 1850, the large 10-road GWR shed at Bath Road was opened for locos in 1934.

Bath Road closed to steam in 1960 and its remaining allocation was moved to St Philip's Marsh (82B) until that, too, closed in 1964 and the remnants were moved to Barrow Road (82E) until closure of that shed in 1965. Bath Road steam shed was replaced by a modern diesel depot with an allocation of 'Warship', 'Western' and 'Hymek' diesel hydraulics, 'Peaks' and, later, Brush Type 4s. This too has closed and all loco servicing is carried out at Barton Hill.

Located on the east side of the south end of Temple Meads station, Bath Road was a difficult shed to visit without a permit but most of its movements could be easily observed from the station. Prior to closure it had an allocation of around 80 locos, many of which were used on main line passenger services to

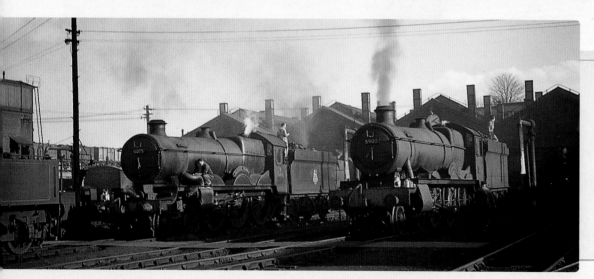

◀ *Another 82A 'Castle' and a 'Grange' get ready for their next turn of duty at Bath Road, c.1959. On the left No. 4075 'Cardiff Castle' was one of the original batch of these fine locos built back in 1924. It was withdrawn in late 1961. On the right is No. 6800 'Arlington Grange', then allocated to Penzance (83G). The first of 80 such locos built at Swindon between 1936 and 1939, this mixed-traffic loco was withdrawn in 1964.*

◀ A night-time shot of the new Bath Road shed taken on August 17, 1963. Already three years old, the diesel depot was home to a number of 'Hymek' (Class 35) and 'Western' (Class 52) diesel hydraulics along with 'Peaks' (Class 45) and Brush Type 4 (Class 47). This shed has now closed and all servicing is carried out at Barton Hill.

Cardiff, Paddington and Exeter. Pride of the fleet were the 20 or so 'Castle' Class 4-6-0s which were kept in tip-top condition for working the crack expresses to Paddington. Star of the show in the late 1950s was No. 7018 'Drysllwyn Castle' – in 1956 the first 'Castle' to be fitted with a double-chimney – which put up electrifying 100 mph performances on the non-stop 'Bristolian'. A fleet of 'Counties' and 'Halls' worked many of the main line and cross-country stopping trains to destinations such as Westbury and Salisbury.

Bath Road's sub-sheds were Bath (closed in 1961), Wells (closed in 1963), Weston-super-Mare (closed in 1960) and Yatton (closed in 1960). Bath and Wells had come under the control of St Philip's Marsh in 1960.

▲ With only just over two months before withdrawal and looking rather neglected without its nameplates, 'Warship' (Class 42) diesel hydraulic No. 829 'Magpie' is seen here at Bath Road on June 14, 1972. Built at Swindon in late 1960, 'Magpie' was withdrawn in August 1972 and cut-up at Swindon in early 1974.

◀ Built by Pressed Steel Co. Ltd, single unit diesel railcar No.W55026 (Class 121) awaits attention at Bath Road in April 1975. At that time it had been working on the Severn Beach branch after transfer from Cardiff Canton and was later to move to Plymouth. Known as 'Bubble Cars', some examples of this class still remain in departmental service.

Exeter St Davids

Designed by Brunel and opened in 1844 by the broad gauge Bristol & Exeter Railway, Exeter St Davids still retains many of its 19th century features including the neighbouring Great Western Hotel.

Exeter St Davids is unique in the UK for having competing services to London departing in the opposite direction to each other – with trains on the former L&SWR route to Waterloo leaving in a southerly direction via Queen Street station (now renamed Central) while trains on the former GWR route to Paddington depart in a northerly direction. In the late 1950s this situation often led to SR 'West Country' or 'Battle of Britain' Pacifics on the 'Atlantic Coast Express' or other holiday trains destined for the 'Withered Arm' rubbing shoulders with WR 'Kings' or 'Castles' on expresses to Paddington or Plymouth and Penzance. In between all of this hustle and bustle were the diminutive WR 1400 Class 0-4-2 tanks on auto-train services up the Exe Valley to Tiverton and Dulverton and SR T9 4-4-0s and Class N 2-6-0s on local services to North Devon and North Cornwall.

Dieselisation of the WR West of England expresses had begun in earnest by 1960 and soon all of these trains were hauled by 'Warship' or 'Western' diesel-hydraulics. 'Hymeks' and the North British Type 2s were also employed on freight and local services. WR steam was ousted by 1963 with the ex-SR lingering on until 1965. Birmingham Railway Carriage & Wagon Co Class 33s were also later employed on the Meldon ballast trains. By 1966 Exeter had been totally dieselised.

▶ The majority of track ballast for the Southern Region came from Meldon Quarry near Okehampton. Here, on May 31, 1961, BR Standard Class 3 2-6-2 tank No. 82023 and 'N' Class 2-6-0 No. 31859 move forward from St Davids with a heavily loaded ballast train to tackle the short 1 in 37 gradient up to Central station. This train was banked in the rear by two of Exmouth Junction's 'Z' Class 0-8-0 tanks, Nos. 30956 and 30955.

▲ A typical bi-regional scene at St Davids on May 25, 1960 as N Class 2-6-0 No. 31834 waits to tackle the incline up to Queen Street with a parcels train. Alongside, 'Warship' Class diesel hydraulic D811 'Daring' waits to depart with the down 'Torbay Express'.

Plymouth North Road

Plymouth North Road station was opened in 1877 and was used by both the GWR and LSWR until 1891 when the latter opened its own terminus at Plymouth Friary.

Plymouth Friary was used by LSWR and, later, SR trains to Exeter via Okehampton until 1958 when the station was closed to passengers and services reverted to using North Road. The latter was then renamed just Plymouth and was completely rebuilt in the early 1960s. Apart from the short section to Bere Alston for Gunnislake branch trains the remainder of the former LSWR route to Exeter via Okehampton was closed in 1966.

Summer Saturdays at North Road saw a succession of holiday trains from London, the Midlands and North bound for Cornwall, headed by 'Castles', 'Halls', 'Granges' and 'Counties'. Many changed engines at Plymouth. A steady stream of china–clay trains heading for the Potteries from St Austell and the famous St Erth to London milk trains were also a regular feature. Seasonal trains carrying potatoes and broccoli from Cornwall also ran, along with branch trains to Launceston via Yelverton usually headed by ex-GWR small 'Prairies'.

Dieselisation of trains on the WR routes started in the late 1950s with the introduction of the (D600) 'Warships' and by the early 1960s all main line trains to Penzance and Paddington were in the hands of the later 'Warships' and 'Westerns' hydraulics. Plymouth Laira closed to steam in April 1964 and dieselisation was complete. By then the dwindling freight services were being hauled by 'Hymeks' and North British Type 2 hydraulics.

▶ Dwarfed by the new Tamar road bridge, 'County' Class 4-6-0 No. 1006 'County of Cornwall' enters Saltash after crossing Brunel's famous Saltash Bridge with the 3.46pm Plymouth to Penzance local on September 7, 1962. No. 1006 was built at Swindon in 1945 and spent most of its life in Cornwall. It was withdrawn from Swindon shed (82C) in September 1963.

▲ Like Exeter St Davids, Plymouth North Road saw the comings and goings of both WR and SR locos. Here, unrebuilt 'Battle of Britain' Class 4-6-2 No. 34079 '141 Squadron' passes through with a milk train in the early 1960s. An Exmouth Junction (72A) loco, this loco was built by BR at Brighton in July 1948 and withdrawn from service in early 1966.

ON SHED
Plymouth Laira
83 D

▼ Castle' Class 4-6-0 No. 5058 'Earl of Clancarty' stands over the ash pits at Laira shed on May 30, 1961. Built at Swindon in 1937, this loco was originally named 'Newport Castle'. Although allocated to 83D at the time of this photo, the 'Earl' was soon to move to Gloucester (85B) from where it was withdrawn in 1963.

Opened by the GWR in 1901, Plymouth Laira was considerably enlarged in 1931. A new diesel depot was opened in 1961 but the steam shed continued to operate until closure in 1964. Located two miles to the east of North Road station, Laira was a 50-minute trek unless a No. 21 Plympton bus was caught from the city centre to Brandon Road. Here, it was but a short stroll to the end of this cul-de-sac and under the railway past the closed Laira Halt to the shed.

Once Laira's diesel depot had opened in 1960 it wasn't long before the shed's steam allocation was hauled off to pastures new or the scrapyard. By October 1961 it was down to a shadow of its former self with a total of only 46 including 2 'Counties', 6 'Castles', 5 'Halls', 1 'Modified Hall', 2 'Kings' and 6 'Granges' and these were all soon destined for withdrawal. The flip

side of the coin at Laira included all five of the original North British 'Warships' (D600-D604), 46 of the new D800 'Warships', 26 of the useless North British Type 2 diesel-hydraulics and the new 'Western' Class hydraulics which were starting to appear from Crewe and Swindon Works.

Laira's only sub-shed was at Launceston (closed 1964) which normally housed a small 'Prairie' for working the branch service to Plymouth via Yelverton.

◄ In May 27, 1962, 'Modified Hall' 4-6-0 No. 6962 'Soughton Hall' rests at Laira after a journey down from its home shed at Old Oak Common (81A). Built at Swindon in 1944 this loco became the first of its class to be withdrawn in early 1963.

▲ On the right No. 6002 'King William IV' alongside North British Type 2 (Class 22) diesel hydraulic D6314. Built in 1927, the 'King' was withdrawn from Stafford Road shed (84A) in 1962. The unreliable Class 22 locos were extinct by 1972.

▲ A diesel hydraulic trio at Laira on March 28, 1970. On the left is 'Warship' D817 'Foxhound' (built Swindon 1960, withdrawn 1971); on the right is another 'Warship' D834 'Pathfinder' (built by North British Loco Co in 1960 and withdrawn in 1971); at the rear is North British Type 2 D6318.

◄ Six 'Western' (Class 52) diesel hydraulics at rest in the gloom of Laira's maintenance bay on April 23, 1974. By this date these fine-looking machines were only just over 10 years old but their non-standard design and unrelibility led to their extinction by 1977. On the left is D1063 'Western Monitor' which was built at Crewe in 1963 and withdrawn from Laira in 1976.

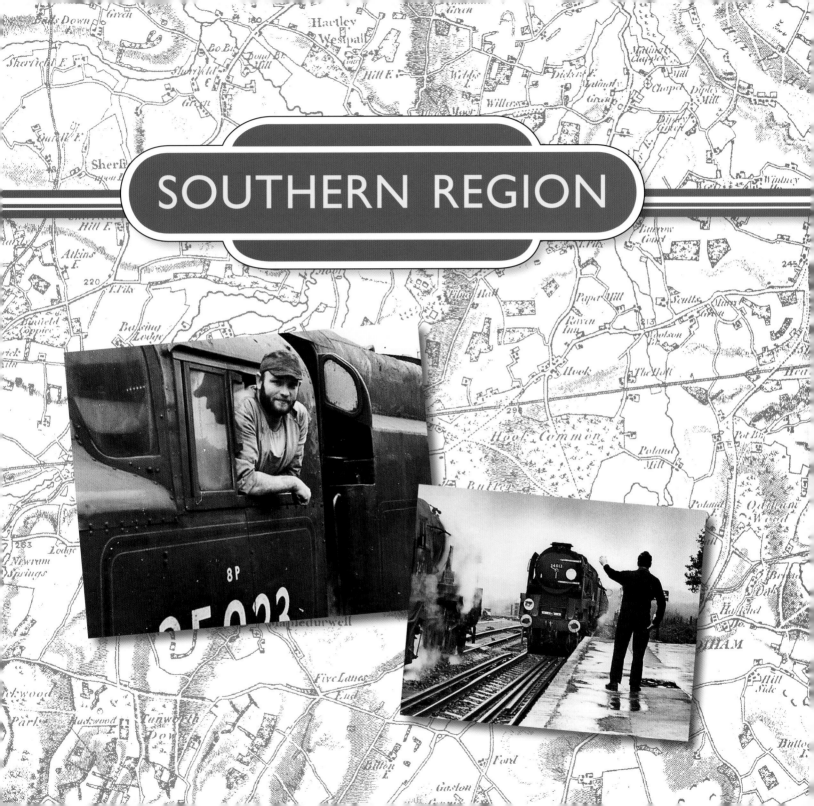

SOUTHERN REGION

London Waterloo

The principal terminus for suburban electric services to south west London and main line services to Portsmouth, Southampton, Bournemouth, Weymouth, and the West of England via Salisbury, Waterloo was opened in 1848 by the London & South Western Railway.

The station was greatly improved and enlarged during the early part of the 19th century, ending up with a total of 21 platforms. Despite third-rail electrification elsewhere on the Southern Region, Waterloo still retained main line steam operations until the summer of 1967 when the Southampton and Bournemouth route was finally 'switched on'.

For the trainspotter in the early 1960s, Waterloo – the last London terminus to see main line steam – was still a romantic place to be, with named trains such as the 'Channel Island Boat Express', 'The Royal Wessex', 'Bournemouth Belle' and the multi-destination 'Atlantic Coast Express' in the capable hands of Bulleid's rebuilt 'Merchant Navy' Class Pacifics. The 'ACE', in summer running in several portions, had through coaches for Ilfracombe, Torrington, Sidmouth, Exmouth, Bude, Padstow and Plymouth. Sadly, it last ran in September 1964 and reduced services between Waterloo, Salisbury and Exeter were gradually handed over to WR 'Warships' and, later, Class 50s, 33s and 47s. Steam, in the form of Bulleid's 'Merchant Navy', 'West Country' and 'Battle of Britain' Pacifics still held sway on Southampton, Bournemouth and Weymouth services until July 1967 when electric multiple units were introduced.

In addition to the named trains, Waterloo regularly witnessed 'Ocean Liner Specials' to and from Southampton Docks Terminus while 'Schools' 4-4-0s and 'H15', 'N15' ('King Arthurs'), 'Lord Nelson' and the named BR Standard Class 5 4-6-0s were also regularly seen hauling summer Saturday trains and local services to Basingstoke and Salisbury. Empty coaching stock was usually handled by Class M7 0-4-4 tanks until the twilight of steam when BR Standard Class 4 and Class 3 tanks were introduced.

▲ Two ex-LSWR Class 'M7' 0-4-4 tanks, Nos. 30123 and 30133 perform empty coaching stock movements at Waterloo in the late 1950s. Designed by Dugald Drummond, 105 of these locos were built between 1897 and 1911, the majority at the company's Nine Elms Works. Initially built to handle suburban services out of Waterloo many eventually found their way to branch line duties in the West Country for which they were fitted for push-pull operation. No. 30123 was built in 1903 and withdrawn from Eastleigh shed (71A) in 1959. No. 30133 was also built in 1903 but was withdrawn from Bournemouth shed (71B) in 1964.

◀ Just arrived at Waterloo from Eastleigh, the first 'Merchant Navy' 4-6-2 to be rebuilt, No. 35018 'British India Line', is seen awaiting inspection from railway officials in February 1956. The remaining 29 'Merchant Navies' had all been rebuilt from their previous 'Spam Can' design by 1960. No. 35018 was originally built at Eastleigh in 1945 and withdrawn in August 1964. It was saved from Woodham's scrapyard at Barry in 1980 after languishing there for nearly 16 years and has since been preserved.

▶ Despite its grimy condition, 'West Country' Class 4-6-2 No. 34038 'Lynton' still manages to attract many admirers at Waterloo station in 1965. It was withdrawn from service in June 1966.

◀ In April 24, 1966, 'Battle of Britain' Class 4-6-2 No. 34064 'Fighter Command' and 'West Country' Class 4-6-2 No. 34032 'Camelford' wait to depart Waterloo with the 9.30am and 9.33am trains for Weymouth respectively.

ON SHED

Nine Elms

70A

Replacing a semi-circular roundhouse, the former LSWR loco shed at Nine Elms consisted of two adjacent sheds – the 'Old Shed' of 15 roads opened in 1885 and the 'New Shed' of 10 roads opened in 1910. Nine Elms, along with nearby Stewarts Lane (73A), which closed in 1963, was the Southern Region's main steam shed in London. The shed provided motive power for all main line services out of Waterloo – to Southampton, Bournemouth, Weymouth and West of England services via Salisbury.

By November 1961 empty coaching stock movements between Clapham and Waterloo were being handled by an allocation of eight M7 0-4-4 tanks and eight WR 0-6-0 pannier tanks. Main line services by then were in the hands of 19 of the very capable BR Standard Class 5 4-6-0s (all carrying names from the withdrawn N15 'King Arthur' Class locos), 12 'West Country' and eight 'Battle of Britain' Class light Pacifics and, to handle the heavyweight expresses such as 'The Bournemouth Belle' and 'Atlantic Coast Express', a total of 12 'Merchant Navy' Pacifics.

▲ *Ex-SR 'Remembrance' Class 4-6-0 No. 32328 'Hackworth' is seen here at Nine Elms in 1950. Designated Class 'N-15X' the seven engines of this class were rebuilds of LBSCR 4-6-4 'Baltic' tanks which were converted by Richard Maunsell in 1934 into 4-6-0 tender engines for hauling expresses on the Waterloo to Southampton line. 'Hackworth' was the first to be withdrawn in 1955 and by 1957 the class was extinct.*

▶ *A scene that has disappeared forever. Three trainspotters - one with regulation duffel bag and another with impractical white trousers - have arrived from Wigan on May 13, 1967 to pay their last respects to Southern steam at Nine Elms. Less than two months later the shed had closed and steam had been eradicated from the region.*

◄ This classic shot of steam at rest was taken at Nine Elms in 1966. Flanked by a BR Standard tank and a rebuilt 'West Country', rebuilt 'Battle of Britain' Class 4-6-2 No. 34077 '603 Squadron' awaits its next turn of duty. Built by BR at Brighton Works in 1948, this loco was rebuilt in 1960 and withdrawn in March 1967.

▲ Despite the removal of its nameplate 'Merchant Navy' Class 4-6-2 No. 35008 ('Orient Line') looks in pretty good shape at Nine Elms on October 7, 1965. Originally built as No. 21C8 at Eastleigh in 1942, this loco was rebuilt in 1957 and withdrawn in July 1967.

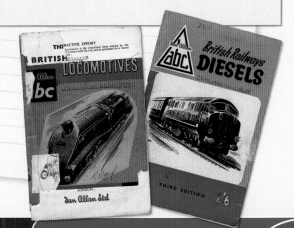

At the same time Nine Elms was still allocated eight of the 'Schools' Class 4-4-0s but these were soon victims of early withdrawal.

For the trainspotter, Nine Elms was located to the south of the main line between Vauxhall and Queens Road stations. Walking time from Wandsworth Road station was about 15 minutes.

Towards the end of its life both the shed and its allocation of steam locos were in a very shabby and rundown condition. It was the last main line steam shed to remain operational in London and, following electrification of the Waterloo to Southampton and Bournemouth lines, it was closed in July 1967. The new Covent Garden fruit and vegetable market was built on its site.

Basingstoke

TOP SPOT

Not exactly a destination on most people's visiting list, but Basingstoke on a summer Saturday in the early 1960s was a trainspotter's paradise.

Not only did we have the spine-tingling spectacle of Bulleid Pacifics thundering through with expresses between Waterloo and Bournemouth, Weymouth and the West Country, but also the slower north-south cross-country services between the Midlands and Bournemouth. Many of the latter worked through to and from Oxford with their SR loco and it was not uncommon to see other workings headed by WR locos such as 'Halls' and 'Granges'. To add to this rich tapestry were the numerous stopping trains, often headed by 'S15's, 'King Arthurs' and named BR Standard Class 5 4-6-0s that took on water at Basingstoke, together with the comings and goings from the nearby shed (70D).

Sadly, the steam-hauled West of England expresses such as the 'Atlantic Coast Express' were withdrawn in September 1964 and 'Warship' diesel-hydraulics – relegated from the WR main line by the new 'Western' diesel-hydraulics– were introduced to haul the much-reduced services. However, the Bournemouth and Weymouth trains continued with steam haulage until July 1967, when that line was electrified as far as Bournemouth Central.

More or less one year apart, two summer-Saturday trainspotting trips to Basingstoke show some interesting results and on both occasions a period of 5½ hours from about 10.30 to 16.00 was spent on the same platform.

August 31, 1963 – a total of 82 locos were recorded, of which ten were Birmingham R. C. & W. Co Type 3 diesels (later Class 33 and known as 'Cromptons'). Of the 72 steam locos seen, 23 were 'West Country', 12 'Battle of Britain', 11 'Merchant Navy' and 11 BR Standard Class 5. WR locos seen on cross-country services were four 'Halls', one 'Grange' and one 'Modified Hall'.

August 22, 1964 – a total of 80 locos were recorded, of which 13 were 'Crompton' diesels and one was a WR 'Warship' (the shape of things to come). Of the 66 steam locos seen, 14 were 'West Country', nine 'Battle of Britain', 14 'Merchant Navy' and 12 BR Standard Class 5. The WR locos seen on cross-country services were two 'Halls', two 'Granges' and two 'Modified Halls'.

▲ Two enthusiasts discuss the run-down state of 'West Country' Class 4-6-2 No. 34093 'Saunton' at Basingstoke in 1966.

► Steam heaven at Basingstoke on 31 August 1963. Just on this page of my notebook I recorded four GWR locos, 23 'Battle of Britain'/'West Country' and 11 'Merchant Navy'. Clinical Basingstoke station doesn't feel the same any more!

34084	6979	76005	✓	✗	✗
34053	34059	35011	✗	✗	✗
34028	34022	6924	✗	✗	✗
34029	34040	73088	✗	✗	✗
35028	35008	76060	✗	✗	✗
73155	34020	30837	✗	✗	✗
73081	75076	73043	✗	✗	✗
34005	34098	31611	✗	✗	✓
6862	D6526	34108	✗	✗	✓
D6524	35001	34031	✓	✗	✗
35002	34104	34047	✗	✗	✗
34056	73115	73080	✗	✗	✗
35020	34042	76067	✗	✗	✗
31787	35006	35030	✗	✗	✗
73084	34009	34079	✓	✗	✗
73016	34075	35009	✗	✗	✗
34005	31864	D6503	✗	✗	✗
73119	35005	35026	✓	✗	✗
34034	73114	34088	✗	✗	✗
D6521	6904	34026	✓	✗	✗

◀ 'Merchant Navy' Class 4-6-2 No. No. 35024 'East Asiatic Company' takes on water at Basingstoke in August 1963 while heading a train for Salisbury. This loco was built at Eastleigh in 1948 and withdrawn at the beginning of 1965 after only 17 years' service.

▶ Headed by 'Merchant Navy' Class 4-6-2 No. 35023 'Holland-Afrika Line', the down 'Bournemouth Belle' is the centre of attention for railway photographers as it speeds through Basingstoke in 1965 – the loco was withdrawn at the end of steam on the SR in July 1967.

Bournemouth

The two stations in Bournemouth, Central and West, had two very different characteristics. Central, a through station, was always the busiest with main line services to Southampton and Waterloo and to Weymouth.

Bournemouth shed (71B) was located just to the west of the station and its allocation in the late 1950s and early '60s included such fine examples as 'N15' 'King Arthurs' and 'LN' 'Lord Nelsons' as well as a clutch of Bulleid Pacifics. By 1962, apart from two 'N15's, the shed was home to 47 other steam locos including 13 'M7' 0-4-4 tanks for working local services including the Swanage branch, 16 'West Countries', two 'Battle of Britains' and eight 'Merchant Navies'. The latter were employed hauling the crack 'Bournemouth Belle' Pullman train which originated at West station and 'The Royal Wessex', half of which originated at West and the other half at Weymouth; both trains united at Bournemouth and destined for Waterloo.

Steam-haulage on this route continued until July 1967 when third-rail electrification was 'switched on'. Electrification of the line to Weymouth was not completed until 1988 and in the intervening years Class 33/1 'Crompton' diesels operated a push-pull service with 4TC unpowered sets. The decrepit state of Central station was finally remedied in 2000 following a programme of extensive refurbishment.

Bournemouth West, a terminus and serviced by Branksome sub-shed, was not only the originating point for many of the Waterloo-bound expresses and local services to Brockenhurst and Salisbury via West Moors, but was also the southern terminus of the Somerset & Dorset Joint Railway services from Bath Green Park. Summer Saturdays were always busy here with 'The Pines Express' from Manchester and other through trains arriving from the north. Loco types on these trains ranged from S&D 7F 2-8-0s and Standard Class 5 4-6-0s to unrebuilt 'West Country' Pacifics and even BR Standard 9F 2-10-0s.

Sadly, through services on the S&D ended in 1962 and what remained, until closure in March 1966, could hardly be called a public service. Bournemouth West station closed for good in the previous October.

▲ While 'M7' Class 0-4-4 No. 30379 tank performs empty coaching stock duties, rebuilt 'West Country' Class 4-6-2 No. 34022 'Exmoor' approaches Bournemouth Central with a Weymouth to Waterloo train on September 8, 1961. 'Exmoor' was built at Brighton in 1946, rebuilt in 1957 and withdrawn in April 1965. On the West Somerset Railway in March 2004 preserved sister engine No. 34027 'Taw Valley' was fitted out with replica name and numberplates from No. 34022 and became 'Exmoor' for the day.

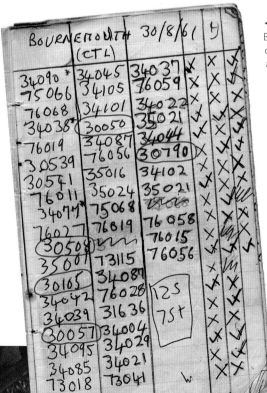

◀ 100% steam at Bournemouth Central on 30 August 1961 with a few old-timers still in action. Of note are Class 'S15' 4-6-0 No. 30508, 'M7' 0-4-4Ts Nos. 30050, 30057 and 30105 and Scotch 'King Arthur' class 4-6-0 No. 30790 'Sir Villiars' – the latter was withdrawn only two months later.

◄ Admired by two young trainspotters rebuilt 'Battle of Britain' Class 4-6-2 No. 34064 'Fighter Command' stands at Bournemouth West after arriving with a stopping train in May 1962. Built at Brighton in 1947, No. 34064 was later fitted with a Giesl Oblong Ejector before being withdrawn in 1966. Terminus of trains from London via Bournemouth Central and from Bath Green Park via the S&DJR, West station closed in October 1965.

▼ A scene that was to soon disappear – trainspotters watch activity at Bournemouth shed from Central station in 1966. With less than a year to go before the end of steam on the SR, BR Standard Class 5 4-6-0 No. 73065 and BR Standard Class 4 2-6-0 No. 76009 are living on borrowed time.

◄ July 3, 1967 – only six days to go before the end of steam on the Southern Region. Driver Prior of Nine Elms shed is seen here at Bournemouth in charge of 'Merchant Navy' Class 4-6-2 No. 35023 'Holland-Afrika Line' with the 11.18am Weymouth to Waterloo express. This loco was built at Eastleigh in 1948, rebuilt in 1957 and withdrawn shortly after this photo was taken.

Located in the fork between the Eastleigh to Southampton and Eastleigh to Portsmouth lines, Eastleigh Works started life in 1891 as a carriage and wagon works for the London & South Western Railway.

▲ *During the 1960s many special trains were organised by railway enthusiast clubs to railway works, sheds and over soon-to-be-closed lines. This one, to Eastleigh Shed and Works, took place on November 11, 1962.*

The railway complex expanded further in 1903 when an engine shed with maintenance and repair facilities was also opened here. The final chapter came in 1910 when all locomotive building was transferred to new workshops at Eastleigh from Nine Elms in London. The locomotives built at Eastleigh under the LSWR's Chief Mechanical Engineers Dugald Drummond and, from 1912, Robert Urie, included, amongst others, 'M7' 0-4-4 tanks and 'H15', 'S15' and 'N15' ('King Arthur' Class) 4-6-0s.

Following the 1923 Grouping, Eastleigh became the principal locomotive works for the Southern Railway and under its new CME, Richard Maunsell, went on to produce the famous 'Lord Nelson' Class 4-6-0s and 'Schools' 4-4-0s. Under Oliver Bulleid, Eastleigh works produced all 30 of the 'Merchant Navy' Class and six of the 'West Country' Class Pacifics – the rest were built at Brighton Works. During World War II Eastleigh even built 23 of the LMS Stanier 8F 2-8-0s. Although Eastleigh ceased building new steam locomotives after Nationalisation, under Southern Region management it rebuilt over 90 of Bulleid's Pacifics between 1956 and 1961. The Works was also heavily involved in building the SR diesel-powered Hastings Units and third-rail electric units and in 1962 built six of the Class 73/0 electro-diesel locomotives.

Although the Works continued to repair steam locos for a few more years, by 1967 and the end of steam on the SR this had ceased completely. Eastleigh continued to repair carriages and multiple units until 2006 when it finally closed.

◀ *A scene inside Eastleigh Works on October 22, 1961. On the left is ex-LBSCR 'K' Class 2-6-0 No. 32343, then allocated to Brighton shed (75A). Designed by L B Billinton a total of 17 of these mixed traffic locos were built between 1913 and 1921. No. 32343 was built at Brighton in 1916 and withdrawn in December 1962. None of this class has been preserved. On the right is ex-L&SWR 'M7' 0-4-4 tank No. 30480 (built 1911) which was then allocated to Eastleigh shed (71A).*

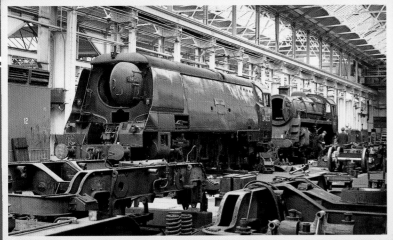

◀ With less than a year to go before the end of steam on the SR, unrebuilt 'West Country' Class 4-6-2 No. 34023 'Blackmoe Vale' undergoes an overhaul at Eastleigh Works on August 21, 1966. Built at Brighton in 1946, this loco was withdrawn in July 1967 and has since been preserved. Behind it a BR Standard Class 4 2-6-0 also receives attention.

▶ A scene soon to disappear for good - unrebuilt 'West Country' Class 4-6-2 No. 34102 'Lapford' and BR Standard Class 4 2-6-0 No. 76008 receive an overhaul at Eastleigh on 24 May 1966. 'Lapford' was built at Eastleigh in 1950 and withdrawn in July 1967. No. 76008 was built at Horwich Works in 1953 and withdrawn from Bournemouth shed (70F) in May 1967.

▼ BR Standard Class 5 4-6-0 No. 73115 rumbles tender-first past Eastleigh Works with a down freight on 24 May 1966. This loco, built only ten years earlier at Doncaster, once carried the name from 'King Arthur' Class 4-6-0 No. 30738 'King Pellinore' (withdrawn in 1958) but the nameplate appears to have been removed by the date of this photo. No. 73115 was finally withdrawn from Guildford shed (70C) in March 1967. Several B. R. C. & W. Co. Type 2 diesels (Class 33/'Cromptons') are in evidence on the right.

Salisbury

TOP SPOT

An important junction, Salisbury was a fascinating station for trainspotters with all SR Waterloo to West of England trains stopping here for water and a steady stream of WR trains arriving from Westbury and Bristol.

Some of these continued on to Portsmouth via Romsey and Eastleigh while Salisbury also saw local stopping services from Bournemouth West via West Moors and from Southampton via Redbridge. There were once two separate stations in Salisbury – one was a terminus served by the GWR (opened 1856) and the other adjacent station (opened 1859) was for L&SWR services between Waterloo and Exeter. The GWR station closed in 1932 and all services subsequently used the present layout.

The fierce competition between the GWR and L&SWR on their competing routes from London to Plymouth Docks in the early 20th century led to the derailment of the 'Ocean Mail' express as it attempted to negotiate Salisbury's curves at speed in 1906. After that date all steam trains, including the famous 'Atlantic Coast Express', were forced to halt at the station.

Steam continued to reign supreme well into the 1960s and in a few hours of trainspotting in September 1963 only two diesel shunters, one 'Hymek' and a three-car Eastleigh diesel-electric set were seen – not a 'Warship' in sight! Even at this late stage nearly all services were steam hauled with Bulleid Pacifics served up alongside 'Halls', 'Granges' and the occasional 'Castle'.

Sadly, with BR regional boundary changes, this was all to change and a year later the last 'ACE' ran and much-reduced services between Exeter and Waterloo were soon in the hands of demoted WR 'Warships'. Steam continued to struggle on until July 1967 when Salisbury shed finally closed.

▲ Ex-SR 'Lord Nelson' Class 4-6-0 No. 30862 'Lord Collingwood' enters Salisbury with a stopping train from Exeter on April 5, 1960. Designed by Richard Maunsell this class of loco was introduced in 1926 for express passenger work on the Waterloo to Exeter main line. 'Lord Collingwood' was built at Eastleigh in 1929 and withdrawn in October 1962. One member of this class, No. 30850 'Lord Nelson', has been preserved.

▲ Salisbury was an important railway crossroads serving both trains on the SR and also to the WR. On September 7, 1961, far from its home shed of Neath (87A), ex-GWR 'Hall' Class 4-6-0 No. 4988 'Bulwell Hall' leaves Salisbury with a cross-country Portsmouth Harbour to Cardiff train. This loco was built at Swindon in 1931 and was withdrawn from Oxford shed (81F) in February 1964.

▶ The arrival of the up and down 'Atlantic Coast Express' always heralded a short but busy time at Salisbury station each day. Here, 'Merchant Navy' Class 4-6-2 No. 35013 'Blue Funnel' is serviced as it heads the up 'ACE' on April 18, 1964. Not only the last stop for this train before Waterloo, Salisbury also saw a change of enginemen, a water refill and the hard work of shovelling coal from the back of the tender to the front. Built at Eastleigh in 1945 'Blue Funnel' was rebuilt in 1956 and withdrawn in July 1967.

▼ Rebuilt 'West Country' Class 4-6-2 No. 34013 'Okehampton' draws out of the down bay platform at Salisbury with the 3.05pm local train to Exeter on April 18, 1964. On the right is station pilot 'M7' 0-4-4 tank No. 30025. Both local engines, 'Okehampton' was built at Brighton in 1945, rebuilt in 1957 and withdrawn in July 1967 while the 'M7' was built in 1899 and withdrawn only six weeks after this photo was taken.

Salisbury

72 B

▲ A grimy BR Standard Class 4 2-6-0 stands on the turntable at Salisbury shed on 20 March 1965.

Not an easy shed to access for the trainspotter unless you could sneak below the foreman's office window, Salisbury shed was located south of the main line west of the station. From here it was about a ten minute walk. The shed provided motive power for local services to Bournemouth, Eastleigh and Portsmouth as well as stopping services west to Exeter and east to Waterloo.

'Foreigners' from the WR via Westbury were also serviced at the shed. Opened by the London & South Western Railway in 1901, by November 1961 it still had 50 steam locos on its books with examples of 11 different classes represented. Some, the 'M7s', 'N15s' ('King Arthurs'), '700s' and 'H15s' were not long for this world, but others, such as its six 'West Countries', six 'Battle of Britains', three 'Merchant Navies' and nine BR Standard Class 3 2-6-0s held on until 1967.

Salisbury shed finally succumbed in July 1967 when the era of steam haulage on the Southern Region finally ended.

◄ Along with a host of SR locos, eight WR steam locos were spotted at Salisbury on September 6, 1963. These included two 'Halls', one 'Modified Hall' and a 'Grange'. 'Castle' Class No. 5073 'Blenheim' was also noted on a train to Bristol.

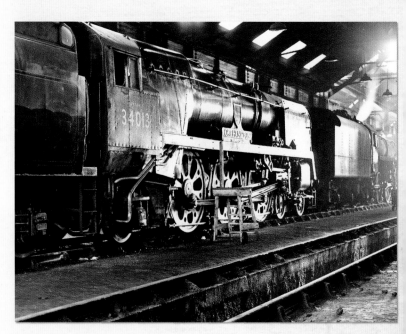

▲ The final year of steam at Salisbury - rebuilt 'West Country' 4-6-2 No. 34013 'Okehampton' is seen at rest inside the shed on August 21, 1966. Less than 12 months later it had been withdrawn and was heading for Cashmore's scrapyard in Newport.

SALISBURY 6TH SEPT. 12

76055	(6338)	31859
4630	76058	(7925)
D2289	D7020	31404
31814	(2883)	30826
76008	31859	34092
34071	35014	34098
(6932)	(6954)	(6809)
31629	34109	35006
(5073)	34095	30828
30841	35025	76054
31857	76656	34078
30021	30508	34101
30309	15234	31802
(4626)	30315	34016
Weymouth	31813	35030
34091	31457	73114
31629	31634	35003
34065	76005	34057
30033	34065	4907
31626	34054	30827

Yeovil Town

72C

Located next to Yeovil Town station, access to this former LSWR shed was very easy through an entrance directly from the station platform. An ex-GWR shed, located at Pen Mill, was closed in 1959 when its allocation was transferred to Yeovil Town. Turntable and servicing facilities were provided at nearby Yeovil Junction which was reached from Town via a spur line. These facilities are used to this day by steam-hauled specials in the 21st century.

Although the shed's allocation was pretty humble, visiting Bulleid light Pacifics from the nearby main line were fairly common. In November 1961 a total of 17 steam locos were allocated to this bi-regional shed, including six WR 0-6-0 pannier tanks, two WR small 'Prairies', two ex-L&SWR M7 0-4-4 tanks and seven 'U' Class Moguls. The WR locos were employed on the local service to Taunton and on shuttle services between Town and Pen Mill station. Recoded 83E under new WR management in 1963, Town shed finally closed in the summer of 1965.

▲ Looking battered but still clinging to life after 66 years' service, ex-LSWR Class '700' No. 30700, formerly of Exmouth Junction shed, was seen in steam at Town shed on December 31, 1963.

▶ Both Westbury and Yeovil Town sheds were 100% steam during a visit on 31 December 1963. At Yeovil, ex-LSWR Class '700' 0-6-0 No. 30700 was surprisingly in steam despite it being officially withdrawn 13 months earlier!

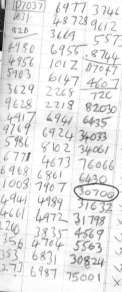

◀ A scene that has disappeared forever - Yeovil Town station and engine shed as seen from the neighbouring farmland on August 17, 1963. In the shed yard is a seemingly motley collection of ex-SR locos including 'S15' 4-6-0s, 'U' 2-6-0s, an unrebuilt 'Battle of Britain' 4-6-2 and a BR Standard Class 4 2-6-4 tank. Also in view is the diminutive steam crane used for loading coal.

Exeter Central

Originally named Queen Street, Central station opened in 1860 as the terminus of the LSWR's main line from Waterloo and Salisbury.

The linking line to Exeter St Davids via a short tunnel and a 1 in 37 gradient was opened in 1862. This allowed LSWR trains to run through to the North Devon and North Cornwall resorts of Ilfracombe, Bude and Padstow and also to Plymouth via what became known as 'The Withered Arm'. Although St Davids was favoured by trainspotters, Central station in the early 60s was still full of interest. It was here that trains such as 'The Atlantic Coast Express' changed engines, with the larger 'Merchant Navy' coming off in favour of a lighter 'West Country' or 'Battle of Britain' for the rest of the journey west – nearby Exmouth Junction shed was allocated an impressive total of 39 Bulleid light Pacifics and seven 'Merchant Navies' in 1962.

Alongside this were the Exmouth branch trains usually hauled by 'M7' 0-4-4 tanks, stopping trains to Salisbury and Barnstaple usually hauled by light Pacifics, freight on the two central roads banked in the rear by a Z Class 0-8-0 tank engine from St Davids and usually hauled by an 'N' Class 2-6-0 with the more heavier ballast trains from Meldon and bulk cement trains in the charge of an 'S15' 4-6-0.

This glorious scene with the trains packed with holidaymakers all ended in September 1964 when the last 'ACE' ran. After that it was all downhill as WR 'Warships' and North British Type 2 diesel-hydraulics took over running of a much-reduced service with the nearby Exmouth Junction shed closing in June 1965.

▲ Ex-LSWR 'T9' 4-4-0 No. 30313 is seen here entering Central Station on August 31, 1960 with a train from Padstow after being banked up the 1 in 37 incline from St Davids by 'Z' Class 0-8-0 tank No. 30955. Known as 'Greyhounds' because of their excellent steaming abilities, 66 of the 'T9' Class were built between 1899 and 1901. No. 30313 was built at Nine Elms Works in 1901 and withdrawn from Exmouth Junction shed (72A) in July 1961.

◀ BR Standard Class 4 2-6-4 tank No. 80064 makes easy going of the 1 in 37 incline up from St Davids station as it approaches Central station with a local passenger train in the 1960s. This loco was built at Brighton in 1953 and has since been preserved as a static display on the Bluebell Line. Note the handshunting of timber wagons on to their turntables on the right of the picture.

◀ Unrebuilt 'Battle of Britain' Class 4-6-2 No. 34076 '41 Squadron' and unrebuilt 'West Country' Class 4-6-2 No. 34034 'Honiton' stand at Exeter Central on September 11, 1959. The 'BB' was built by BR in 1948 and withdrawn in January 1966, the 'WC' was built in 1946 and withdrawn in July 1967.

▶ Complete with eight-wheel tender Class 'S15' 4-6-0 No. 30829 arrives at Exeter Central with a train of empty ballast hoppers en route to Meldon Quarry on August 1, 1962. One of ten such locos then allocated to Salisbury (72B) these powerful goods locos were also employed on stopping passenger services. Although all had been withdrawn by 1966 seven have since been preserved.

Exmouth Junction

72 A

▲ Unrebuilt 'West Country' Class 4-6-2 No. 34030 'Watersmeet' was seen outside Exmouth Junction shed on September 1, 1964. This loco was built at Brighton in 1946 and withdrawn shortly after being photographed here.

Located over a mile to the east of Exeter Central station and north of the junction between the main line to Salisbury and the Exmouth branch, Exmouth Junction shed was best approached from Polsloe Bridge Halt from which it was about a ten minute walk. One of the largest on the Southern Region, the first shed here was opened by the LSWR in 1887. This was closed in 1927 when a new 12-road shed was opened on an adjacent site. With an allocation of over 100 locos, the shed provided motive power not only for top link duties such as the 'Atlantic Coast Express' and other main line services to Salisbury, North Devon and North Cornwall along the 'Withered Arm', but also for the many SR branch lines in the area. For years Exmouth Junction was also home to the entire class of 'Z' Class 0-8-0 tanks which were employed on banking duties between St Davids and Central station.

Even as late as November 1961 Exmouth Junction's allocation of steam locos totalled 123, but by then more modern ex-LMS and BR standard types had replaced many of the older LSWR engines such as the 'T9'

◄ Exmouth Junction shed still held on to a large allocation of SR locos in August 1963. Of the 40 locos seen on shed on the 8th of that month ten were Bulleid light Pacifics and five were 'Merchant Navies'. Ivatt Class 2 2-6-2 tanks, replacing the older 'M7' and Adams Radial tanks, were also common.

▲ Unrebuilt 'Battle of Britain' Class 4-6-2 No. 34080 '74 Squadron' is seen here on Exmouth Junction's turntable shortly before withdrawal in 1964. By this date Southern steam at Exeter was on its way out and soon to be replaced by WR diesel-hydraulics. No. 34080 was built by BR at Brighton in 1948 and was withdrawn in September 1964.

A line-up of Bulleid unrebuilt Pacifics at Exmouth Junction shed in the early 1960s. All three were built at Brighton Works, from left to right: 'Battle of Britain' Class No. 34065 'Hurricane' (built 1947, withdrawn April 1964); 'West Country' Class No. 34023 'Blackmore Vale' (built 1946, withdrawn July 1967 and since preserved); 'Battle of Britain' Class No. 34073 '249 Squadron' (built by BR in 1948, withdrawn June 1964).

4-4-0s and Class '700' 0-6-0s. Only six of the 'M7' 0-4-4 tanks remained but there were 15 of the Ivatt Class 2 2-6-2 tanks and ten of the BR Standard Class 3 2-6-2 tanks, many of which were employed on branch lines such as Axminster to Lyme Regis. Freight trains and some local passenger services to North Devon and North Cornwall were mainly in the charge of 28 Class 'N' 2-6-0s, while freight towards Salisbury was handled by six 'S15' 4-6-0s. Primarily, Exmouth Junction had a massive allocation of 46 Bulleid Pacifics, nearly 50% more than Nine Elms. Of these 39 were the lighter 'West Country' and 'Battle of Britain' classes which were ideally suited for both main line services to Salisbury and on the lines to North Devon and Plymouth and North Cornwall via Okehampton. Heavier expresses east of Exeter, such as 'The Atlantic Coast Express' were in the capable hands of seven 'Merchant Navies'.

The shed's code was changed to 83D in 1963 when the Western Region took responsibility for all former SR routes west of Salisbury and for a short time ex-GWR locos were also based at Exmouth Junction. Exmouth Junction's far-flung empire included sub-sheds at Bude (closed 1964), Callington (closed 1964), Exmouth (closed 1963), Lyme Regis (closed 1965), Okehampton (closed 1964) and Seaton (closed 1963). Exmouth Junction closed to steam in 1965 when most duties were taken over by relegated WR 'Warships' and North British Type 2 diesel hydraulics.

▲ Far from its home at Aberdeen Ferryhill (61B), 'A4' Class 4-6-2 No. 60024 'Kingfisher' takes on water at Exmouth Junction on March 27, 1966. This much-travelled loco was heading the Locomotive Club of Great Britain (LCGB) 'A4 Commemorative Railtour' to the West Country. By this date the shed had already closed to steam but had obviously retained basic servicing facilities.

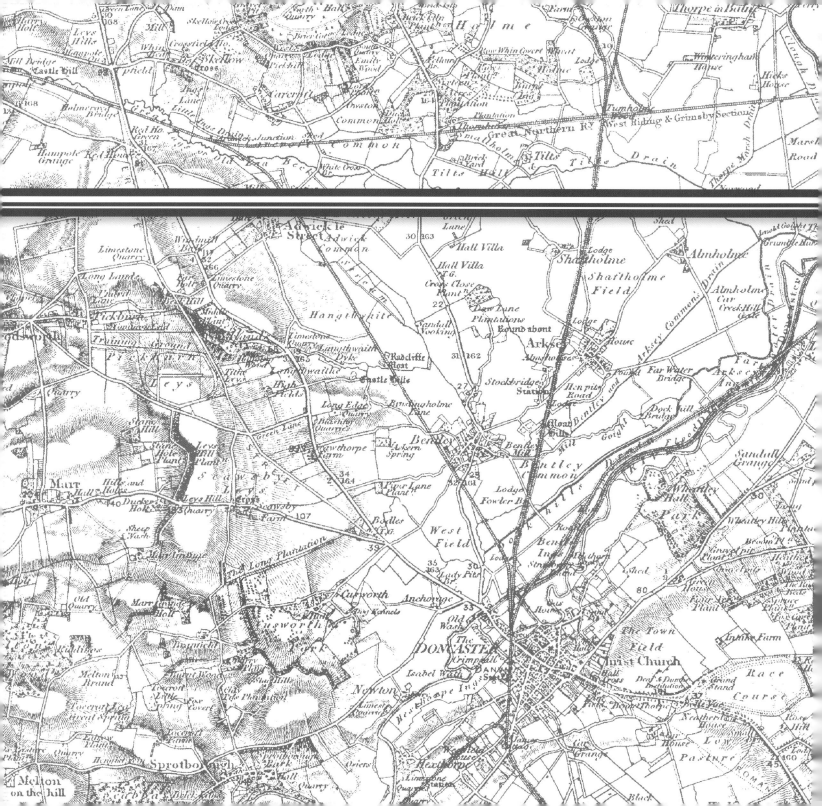

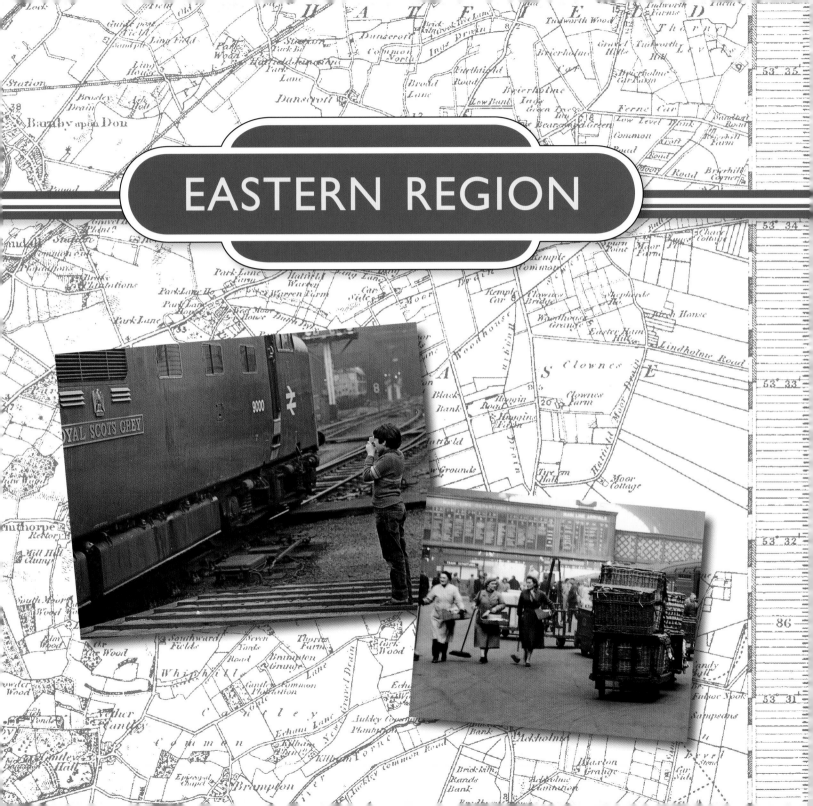

EASTERN REGION

London Liverpool St

Opened by the Great Eastern Railway as its main London terminus in 1874, Liverpool Street had become an early victim of dieselisation and electrification by 1960.

Prior to that and despite some early electrification of lines to Shenfield and Chelmsford, the station's 18 platforms were busy with the comings and goings of the numerous 'N7' 0-6-2 and 'J67' 0-6-0 tanks on the intensive suburban services. Main line services to Cambridgeshire, Essex, Suffolk and Norfolk were in the hands of Class 'B17' 'Sandringham' 4-6-0s (of which two were streamlined until 1951), Class 'B12' 4-6-0s, Class 'B1 4-6-0s and, last but not least, the BR Standard Class 7MT 'Britannia' 4-6-2s which had started coming on stream in the early 1950s. These superb locos, of which 21 were allocated to Norwich by 1958, handled many of the top link services such as the 'Hook Continental' and 'The Norfolkman' out of Liverpool Street.

Other named trains leaving Liverpool Street in the early '60s included 'The Essex Coast Express', 'The East Anglian', and 'The Broadsman'. The introduction of English Electric Type 4 (Class 40) diesels in 1958 meant that there were only three 'Britannias' left on these services by 1961. Brush Type 2 (Class 31), soon joined by the English Electric Type 3 (Class 37) diesels, had already taken over many of the other steam-hauled services and by 1962 all main line services from Liverpool Street were diesel-hauled. The main steam shed for the area, Stratford (30A) had also closed by September of that year. A visit to Liverpool Street in August 1965 revealed all of the above diesel classes plus a number of Brush Type 4 (Class 47) diesels and empty coaching stock in the hands of short-lived BTH Type 1 (Class 15) diesels. The diesel picture was complete – but not for long, as by 1986 the electrified main line to Norwich was 'switched on', followed by the Cambridge line in 1987 and King's Lynn in 1992.

▲ A portrait of contrasts under the wires – until the early dieselisation of the Great Eastern line out of Liverpool Street, Stratford shed always turned out their 'N7' 0-6-2 tanks in immaculate condition for both suburban and station pilot duties. Shortly before withdrawal in 1960, Class 'N7/4' No. 69614 makes a perfect contrast to the recently arrived Brush Type 2 (Class 31) D5571.

▶ If it weren't for the then-modern diesel, this scene at Liverpool Street could have been taken in the 1930s. D5512, one of the first batch of Brush Type 2 diesels (Class 31) to be delivered to the ER from Loughborough in 1957–58, waits for laundry baskets to be loaded into a Gresley parcels van in March 1959.

Class 'B17/6' No. 61656 'Leeds United' arrives at Liverpool Street with an express from Yarmouth in April 1958. On the left 'Britannia' Class 4-6-2 No. 70003 'John Bunyan' waits to depart with an express for Norwich. The 'B17' (or 'Sandringham') was built in 1936 and withdrawn in January 1960. No. 70003 was built at Crewe in 1951 and spent the first half of its life working on the Great Eastern main line between Liverpool Street and Norwich. Displaced by English Electric Type 4 (Class 40) diesels this loco ended its days at Carlisle Kingmoor from where it was withdrawn in March 1967.

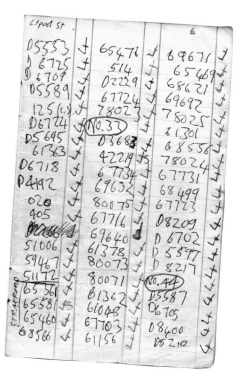

▲ A mega shed bash around London on September 4, 1962 included a visit to Liverpool Street Station and Stratford. While the former was by now 100% diesel, Stratford shed still had a vast array of both steam and diesel locos. Of interest at Stratford were Departmental Locomotives No. 33 (LNER 'Y4' Class 0-4-0T No. 68129) and No. 44 (ex-LNER 'Class 'J69' 0-6-0T No. 68498.

ON SHED

Stratford

30 A

By far the shed with the biggest allocation in the UK, at one stage in the early 1950s Stratford boasted nearly 400 locos, nearly half of which were 'N7' 0-6-2 and 'J67' and 'J69' 0-6-0 tanks used for the intensive suburban service out of Liverpool Street. Dispersed over a wide area, the shed and the adjoining ex-GER works were a 10-minute walk from Stratford station. By 1960 a new diesel depot had been opened and the steam shed reduced in size. Following the early electrification of suburban lines and the dieselisation of other services the remaining steam locos at Stratford had become redundant by 1962. Once famous as the home to many ex-LNER

▲ Seen here at Stratford shed c.1959, Thompson 'L1' Class 2-6-4 tank No. 67716 was one of 100 such locos that were introduced between 1945 and 1950. Sadly, the class was short-lived due to its poor steaming abilities and unreliability. Allocated to Stratford, No. 67716 was built at Darlington in 1948 and saw service on suburban passenger trains from Liverpool Street to Hertfordshire.

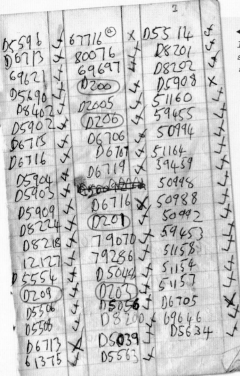

◄ Away from the long lines of withdrawn steam locos, Stratford shed on September 4, 1962 was nearly 100% dieselised. The exceptions were a solitary 'B1' 4-6-0, two 'N7' 0-6-2 tanks a 'L1' 2-6-4 tank and a BR Standard Class 4 2-6-4 tank. Five of the original batch of English Electric Type 4 (Class 40) diesels, D200, D201, D203, D206 and D209, were also on shed.

4-6-0 types employed on main line services out of Liverpool Street including 'B1', B12/3' and B17' ('Sandringham') Classes, by November 1961 the steam allocation was reduced to a shadow of its former self with only 47 locos. This included 11 'B1' 4-6-0s, seven of the ancient 'J15' 0-6-0s, nine 'L1' 2-6-4 tanks, the remaining 11 members of the 'J69' 0-6-0 tanks and nine of the once numerous 'N7' 0-6-2 tanks. Departmental steam locos allocated to Stratford Works were two 'J69' tanks, a 'J66' 0-6-0 tank and a 'Y4' 0-4-0 saddle tank.

By 1962 Stratford was growing from strength to strength with an allocation of 171 diesel locos. These included the first ten of the English Electric Type 4 (Class 40), 29 of the English Electric Type 3 (Class 37), 56 of the Brush Type 2 (Class 31) and two types of very unsuccessful locos – the entire class of ten of the North British Type 1 (Class 16) and 16 of the British Thomson-Houston Class 1 (Class 15). Even this impressive line-up has since been dispatched to the breaker's yard, and the diesel shed and the railway works have all gone.

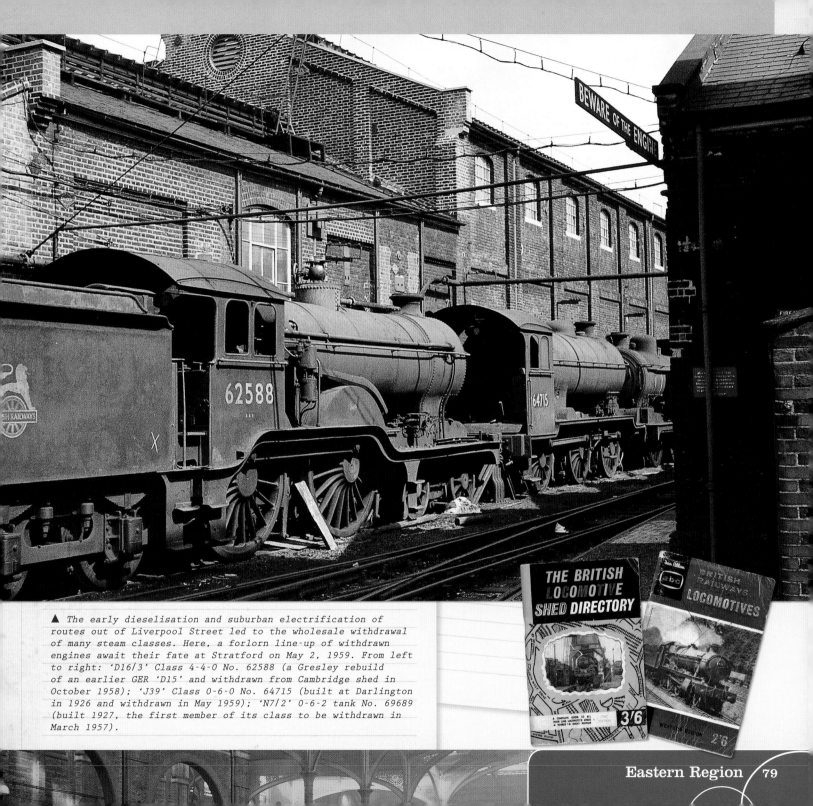

BEWARE OF THE ENGINE

62588

64715

▲ *The early dieselisation and suburban electrification of routes out of Liverpool Street led to the wholesale withdrawal of many steam classes. Here, a forlorn line-up of withdrawn engines await their fate at Stratford on May 2, 1959. From left to right: 'D16/3' Class 4-4-0 No. 62588 (a Gresley rebuild of an earlier GER 'D15' and withdrawn from Cambridge shed in October 1958); 'J39' Class 0-6-0 No. 64715 (built at Darlington in 1926 and withdrawn in May 1959); 'N7/2' 0-6-2 tank No. 69689 (built 1927, the first member of its class to be withdrawn in March 1957).*

THE BRITISH LOCOMOTIVE SHED DIRECTORY

A COMPLETE GUIDE TO ALL MAIN LINE LOCOMOTIVE SHEDS & WORKS IN GREAT BRITAIN

3/6

abc BRITISH RAILWAYS LOCOMOTIVES

WESTERN REGION

2'6

London King's Cross

Designed by Lewis Cubitt, King's Cross station was opened in 1852 as the London terminus of the Great Northern Railway.

I n addition to handling the intensive north London suburban services the station was also the starting point for expresses up the East Coast Main Line via York and Newcastle to Edinburgh and Aberdeen. The most famous of these were the 'Flying Scotsman' and the pre-war 'Silver Jubilee', but others during BR days included the 'Elizabethan', 'Aberdonian', 'Queen of Scots', 'Talisman' and the 'Tyne-Tees Pullman'.

Haulage of these top link trains was in the capable hands of King's Cross shed's (34A) allocation of Class 'A3' and 'A4' Gresley Pacifics, but regular 'foreign' locos included Peppercorn Class 'A1' Pacifics and, towards the end of steam, Immingham-based 'Britannia' Pacifics. Gresley Class 'V2' 2-6-2s and Thompson Class 'B1' 4-6-0s were also often employed on passenger duties during peak holiday periods.

Suburban services including those to Moorgate were handled by King's Cross shed's large allocation of Class 'L1' 2-6-4 and 'N2' 0-6-2 tanks. By 1962 diesel multiple units, 'Baby Deltics' (Class 23) and Brush Type 2s (Class 31) had taken over suburban services. However, in April of that year – only just over a year before the end of steam at King's Cross – the station was still a great place for the trainspotter with, in the space of a few hours, Classes 'A1', 'A3', 'A4', 'V2' and 'Britannia' all being spotted.

Steam was in about equal numbers to the diesels seen, these coming mainly from Finsbury Park shed (34G) and including English Electric Type 4 (Class 40), 'Deltic' (Class 55), Brush Type 2 (Class 31), BR Sulzer Type 2 (Class 24) and the short-lived 'Baby Deltics' (Class 23). Steam operations ended in June 1963 when King's Cross shed was closed and diesels continued to reign until electrification of the ex-GNR line between 1976 and 1991.

▲ A classic scene of Gresley Pacifics at King's Cross bufferstops in 1962 – 'A3' Class No. 60109 'Hermit' and record-breaking 'A4' No. 60022 'Mallard' have just arrived with trains from the north. Both King's Cross shed (34A) locos, No. 60109 was built in 1923 as an LNER 'A1' Class, rebuilt as an 'A3' in 1943 and withdrawn in November 1962. No. 60022, holder of the world speed record for steam locos of 126 mph, was built in 1938 and withdrawn in April 1963. It has since been preserved as part of the National Collection.

▼ 'V2' Class 2-6-2 No. 60854 and 'A3' Class 4-6-2 No. 60065 'Knight of Thistle' simmer at the buffer stops on May 4, 1963 after arriving with trains from the north. The 'A3', fitted with a round dome and German-style smoke deflectors, was built as an LNER 'A1' Class at Doncaster in 1924, rebuilt as an 'A3' in 1947 and withdrawn in June 1964.

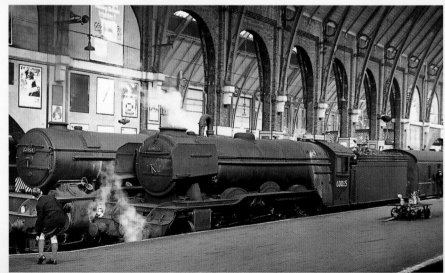

◄ A scene full of detail taken from above the stabling point at King's Cross station on 20 June 1959 – in view are two 'A4s' and an arriving 'A3' while at the end of Platform 1 are the usual group of young trainspotters.

▼ King's Cross in the last years of steam – watched by a few young spotters, Peppercorn 'A1' 4-6-2 No. 60136 'Alcazar' arrives with an express from Edinburgh in May 1962. Then allocated to Doncaster (36A), this fine loco was less than 15 years old when it was withdrawn in May 1963.

◄ The visit to London on 4 September 1962 also included a lively sojourn at King's Cross station – here we have two 'Baby Deltics', two 'Deltics', two 'Britannias', two 'A1s', one 'A4', one 'V2' and two 'A3s'. Steam disappeared from King's Cross just over nine months later.

London King's Cross

34 A

Home, until the end of steam, to such famous locos as 'Flying Scotsman' and 'Mallard', King's Cross shed was originally opened by the Great Northern Railway in 1851 and under both LNER and BR ownership went through several changes before finally succumbing to the diesel invasion when it closed in June 1963.

Located in King's Cross goods yard, the shed was about 15 minutes' walk north from King's Cross station. As the Eastern region's top link shed, King's Cross provided motive power for many of the East Coast Main Line expresses and for the intensive suburban services to north London and Hertfordshire. With the new diesel depot at Finsbury Park coming on stream in 1960, by November 1961 King's Cross shed's allocation was down to 53 steam locos, having already lost most of its 'L1' and 'N2' suburban tanks due to the early dieselisation of the suburban services.

However, even at this late stage and with the 'Deltic' onslaught already underway the shed could still muster an impressive line-up of 19 'A4' and 11 'A3' Gresley Pacifics, plus seven 'B1' 4-6-0s and eight 'V2' 2-6-2s. At the same time Finsbury Park was allocated 99 main line diesels including six 'Deltics' (Class 55), 40 Brush Type 2 (Class 31) and 25 BR Sulzer Type 2 (Class 24).

▲ *A powerful line-up at King's Cross shed in 1959 - Peppercorn 'A1' 4-6-2 No. 60153 'Flamboyant' (built Doncaster 1949, withdrawn November 1962) and 'A4' No. 60034 'Lord Faringdon' (built Doncaster 1938, originally named 'Peregrine', withdrawn August 1966). The 'A1' was one of five of this class fitted with Timken roller bearings which totally transformed their performance, reliability and mileage between general overhauls.*

▶ *The shed yard at King's Cross in the days when engine shed security was somewhat more lax than today and spotters could get closer to the engines they so admired. The object of the boy photographer's attention on 27 July 1960 appears to be the appearance of Edinburgh Haymarket Class 'A3' No. 60037 'Hyperion', a rare sight at Kings Cross if ever there was one. Also in attendance is 'A3' No. 60059 'Tracery', 'A4' No. 60025, 'Falcon' bearing 'The Elizabethan' headboard, 'A4' No. 60014 'Silver Link', complete with 'Flying Scotsman' headboard and another, unidentified A4. What a line up!*

▲ A steamy line-up of Pacifics at King's Cross shed in 1960. From left to right: 'A4' No. 60014 'Silver Link' (the first 'A4', built 1935, withdrawn end of 1962); 'A2/3' No. 60519 'Honeyway' (built 1947, withdrawn end of 1962); 'A4' No. 60003 'Andrew K. McCosh' (originally named 'Osprey', built 1937, withdrawn end of 1962); 'A2/3' No. 60512 'Steady Aim' (built 1946, withdrawn June 1965) and an unidentified Peppercorn 'A1'.

◄ Looking in good fettle, Class 'A3' 4-6-2 No. 60055 'Woolwinder' is coaled up in readiness for its next turn of duty from its home shed, c.1960. Built as an LNER 'A1' in 1924 and named after the 1907 St Leger winner, 'Woolwinder' spent much of its life on the Great Central main line. Here it is seen fitted with a double Kylchap exhaust system and experimental smoke-deflecting 'fins', shortly before withdrawal in September 1961.

Doncaster

Doncaster was a fabulous spot for trainspotters in the 1950s and early 60s. Not only did it sit astride the East Coast Main Line and was the location of the famous Doncaster Works, but was also a major junction for Humberside, north Lincolnshire and the industrial heart of Yorkshire.

Until dieselisation of the East Coast Main Line the station was alive with the comings and goings of 'A1s', 'A2s', 'A3s' and 'A4s' heading south to King's Cross or north to Leeds, York, Newcastle and Edinburgh with their important expresses. However, by 1963 the arrival of the English Electric Type 4 (Class 40), BR Sulzer Type 4 (Class 46) and 'Deltic' (Class 55) diesels had brought about the demise of steam on these services. Despite this, steam locos – albeit in ever-decreasing numbers – continued to be used for a few more years on the heavy goods trains from the Yorkshire coalfields and the massive steel works at Scunthorpe. Dieselisation was complete in May 1966 when Doncaster shed (36A) closed – the last to do so on the Eastern Region.

Even as late as August 1965 a short stay (arrived 11.19, departed 13.50) on the platforms at Doncaster station revealed in just that time three 'B1' 4-6-0s, one '04/8' 2-8-0, eight 'exWD 2-8-0s and two BR 9F 2-10-0s in action on freight trains.

▲ Photographed in the original BR livery soon after delivery from Darlington Works in 1949, Peppercorn Class 'A1' 4-6-2 No. 60144 pauses at Doncaster with an up train. A local engine (36A) for most of its life, No. 60144 was later named 'King's Courier' and was withdrawn from Doncaster shed in April 1963.

▶ Watched by a gaggle of spotters, ex-LNER 'J39' Class No. 64840 waits to leave Doncaster with a local stopping train in June 1954. Although one of Gresley's less handsome locos, the 'J39' Class was the most numerous with 289 being built between 1926 and 1941. No. 64840 was built at Darlington in 1932 and withdrawn from Ardsley shed (56B) in November 1962.

◀ With a backdrop of Doncaster Works (known as 'The Plant'), Class A2/3 4-6-2 No. 60523 'Sun Castle' heads out of Doncaster station with an up express for King's Cross on 29 November 1962

▶ Gresley 'V2' Class 2-6-2 No. 60983 passes through Doncaster's middle road with an up empty coaching stock train in August 1961. One of 184 powerful and versatile 'V2' locos introduced between 1936 and 1944, this loco was built at Darlington in 1944 and withdrawn from Grantham shed (34F) in September 1962.

▲ By August 1965 the Doncaster area was the last outpost of steam in the Eastern Region. A circuitous trip from King's Lynn via Peterborough and the ECML on August 13th included a one-hour stopover at Doncaster before returning via Scunthorpe, Grimsby, Louth and Boston. A total of 26 steam freight locos were seen in action in the Doncaster and Scunthorpe area including 14 ex-WD 2-8-0, six 'B1' 4-6-0, two 'O4' 2-8-0, two BR Standard '9F' 2-10-0. Two 'K1' 2-6-0 Nos 62035 and 62067 were seen in action between Scunthorpe and Grimsby.

Opened by the Great Northern Railway in 1853, Doncaster Works went on to build some of the world's finest steam locomotives.

▲ *Peppercorn 'A1' Class 4-6-2 No. 60123 'H. A. Ivatt' at Doncaster Works on September 29, 1962. The loco had been involved in an accident at Offord on the ECML south of Huntingdon earlier that month, and in October it became the first 'A1' to be withdrawn from service. When only eight months old, No. 60123 was also involved in an accident at Lincoln.*

UNDER THE GNR'S Chief Mechanical Engineers, firstly Patrick Stirling then Henry Ivatt (from 1896) and Nigel Gresley (from 1911), Doncaster Works produced, among others, the famous Stirling Singles, Ivatt Atlantics and Gresley Pacifics. The first two of the original 'A1' Class Pacifics were introduced in 1922 and a year later the GNR was absorbed into the LNER.

A total of 52 of these locos were built before being rebuilt as 'A3' Pacifics, with another 27 of the latter being built from new. These were followed by 35 of the world-famous 'A4' Pacifics, including the holder of the world steam record, 'Mallard', and batches of the highly successful 'V2' 2-6-2 mixed traffic locos. Thompson's A2/2 and Peppercorn's A2 and a batch of A1 Pacifics followed, with many of the latter built after Nationalisation under the new British Railways management.

Under BR the Works (nicknamed the 'Plant') went on to build 42 of the BR Standard Class 5 4-6-0s, 70 of the Class 4 2-6-0s (of which No. 76114 was the last steam loco to be built at Doncaster when completed on 31 October 1957) and ten of the Class 4 2-6-4 tanks. By 1957 Doncaster had produced over 2,000 steam locos. Diesel loco construction followed with batches of Classes 03, 08 and 10 diesel-shunters, 84 of the Class 56 and 50 of Class 58 diesels.

Doncaster had also built the prototype Class EM1 electric locomotive (later Class 76) for the 1.5 kV DC Woodhead line back in 1941. Production of electric locos was resumed in 1958 with 24 of the 750 V DC third rail Class 71 (E5000-E5023) for the Southern Region and, starting in 1961, 40 of the Class 85 and 60 of Class 86 25kV Ac locos for the West Coast Main Line. The 'Plant' celebrated its 150th anniversary in July 2003.

◄ *Doncaster Works, Crimsal Erecting Shop, on June 19, 1947 - not quite British Railways but only just over six months to go before Nationalisation. A Thompson 'B1' 4-6-0 and a Gresley 'A3' 4-6-2 receive heavy-duty attention as the sun streams through the soot-stained windows. This famous building was demolished in 2008 and replaced by a modern housing development.*

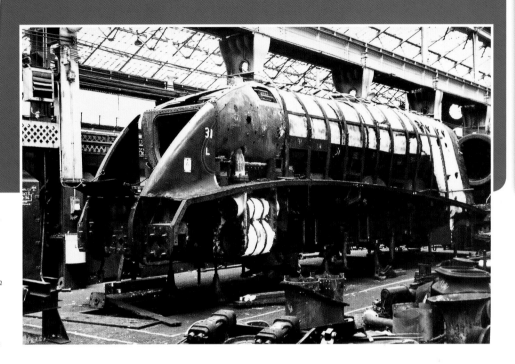

DONCASTER WORKS & SHED
ALSO YORK SHED & MUSEUM

SUNDAY 11th OCTOBER

MERCHANT NAVY PACIFIC

From	
BIRMINGHAM (New St.)	FARE
BURTON-ON-TRENT	45/-
DERBY (Midland)	

BUFFET CAR

OUTWARD via SHEFFIELD, DONCASTER & SELBY
RETURN via CHURCH FENTON & SHEFFIELD

Tickets and full details f...

▶ A4' Class 4-6-2 No. 60031 'Golden Plover' is undergoing overhaul at the 'Plant' (the loco's birthplace in 1937), photographed during a visit organised by the Home Counties Railway Society on September 9, 1963. Although steam locomotive construction ended at Doncaster in October 1957, the overhaul of main line steam continued into the 1960s. 'Golden Plover', allocated to St Rollox (65B), was undergoing its last overhaul before withdrawal in November 1965.

▼ The end of the road for two Gresley Class 'N2' 0-6-2 tanks. Nos. 69557 and 69566 were on Doncaster's scrap line in 1957. Introduced by the GNR in 1920 many of these sturdy locos could be found hard at work on King's Cross suburban trains until withdrawal in the late 1950s.

Doncaster

36 A

Not only one of the largest sheds in the Eastern Region, Doncaster was also one of the last to close to steam. In addition to providing top link motive power for the East Coast Main Line, Doncaster shed also provided heavy freight locos for the local coal and steel traffic in this heavily industrial area of south Yorkshire.

About a 20-minute walk south from Doncaster Station, the shed was originally opened by the Great Northern Railway in 1876. By the late 1950s its allocation was just under 200 locos but, even with the increasing dieselisation of main line services, by November 1961 it was still home to a staggering 155 steam locos plus 19 0-6-0 diesel shunters. Twelve different classes were represented including 13 'A1' and three 'A2' Pacifics, 22 'V2' 2-6-2s, 25 'B1' 4-6-0s, 16 'K1'/'K3' 2-6-0s and for heavy freight 20 'O2/O4' 2-8-0s, 30 ex-WD 2-8-0s and 16 BR Standard '9F' 2-10-0s.

The shed finally closed to steam in May 1966 but continued to serve as a diesel depot.

▲ Contrasting giants at Doncaster Motive Power Depot in 1964 featuring (left) ex-GCR Robinson 'O4' Class 2-8-0 No. 63613 rebuilt with a 'B1' type round-topped boiler and a pair of ex-W D 'Austerity' 2-8-0s, including No. 90305. These two classes alone originally totalled 1,254 engines – an indication of the vast freight traffic once handled by Britain's railways.

▼ This view of the south end of Doncaster shed was taken on June 9, 1963. Along with ex-WD 2-8-0, BR '9F' 2-10-0, 'B1' 4-6-0 and a Brush Type 4 (class 47) diesel are Peppercorn 'A1' Class 4-6-2 No. 60124 'Kenilworth' (built Doncaster 1949, withdrawn March 1966) on the left and, left of centre 'A1' Class No. 60149 'Amadis' (built Darlington 1949, withdrawn June 1964). BR Standard 'Britannia' 4-6-2 No. 70008 'Black Prince' (built Crewe 1951, withdrawn January 1967) was visiting from March shed (31B).

▶ The surrounding coalfields gave rise to Doncaster having a large allocation of ex-WD 'Austerity' 2-8-0s. This scene, taken on a Sunday afternoon in 1964, shows six of these classic heavy freight machines waiting to resume their diagrams the following morning.

◀ A smoky scene in Doncaster shed in 1963 depicting 'War Department' 2-8-0 No. 90484 - one of 33 still allocated there in May 1965. After World War II the 'dub-dee' spent its life working in the Doncaster area and was withdrawn from that shed in May 1966. On the left is a former Great Central '04' Class 2-8-0 rebuilt with a round-top boiler.

Norwich Thorpe

ON SHED

32 A

Located about a 10-minute walk east of Norwich Thorpe station, this shed was opened by the Yarmouth & Norwich Railway in 1844. Further improvements were carried out by the LNER in the 1930s but the early dieselisation of services in East Anglia had brought about the end of steam by the early 1960s. The shed's heyday was in the 1950s when around 80 steam locos were allocated here including the classic 'D16' 4-4-0s, 'B12', 'B17' ('Sandringhams') and 'B1' 4-6-0s.

However, pride of place must go to the 21 BR Standard Class 7MT 'Britannia' Pacifics (including 70000 herself) which did such sterling service on expresses to London Liverpool Street. Sadly, with the onslaught of the Brush Type 2 (Class 31) and English Electric Type 4 (Class 40) diesels, by November 1961 there were only three 'Britannias' left, with the rest having been reallocated to March (31B). In fact, on closure to steam in April of that year, Norwich Thorpe's allocation of steam locos had dwindled to only 16, of which seven were ex-GER 'J17' and 'J19' 0-6-0s.

Sub-sheds of Norwich Thorpe were Cromer Beach (closed 1959), Dereham (closed 1955) and Wymondham (closed 1958).

▲ *Photographed on August 29, 1959, exactly one month before withdrawal, Class 'B17/6' 4-6-0 No. 61612 'Houghton Hall' of Ipswich shed (32B) was still alive and kicking at Norwich shed. Built at Darlington as a 'B17' in 1930, No. 61612 was rebuilt as a 'B17/6' in 1950. In total 73 locos of this class were built and all were named, either after English country houses or football clubs. In 1937 two members of this class (No. 61659 'East Anglian' and No. 61670 'City of London') were given streamlined casings similar in appearance to the 'A4'. The casing was removed in 1951.*

▶ *Norwich Thorpe shed was famous for its allocation of 'Britannia' Pacifics. By 1960, when this photo was taken, with the introduction of English Electric Type 4 (Class 40) diesels on the GEML the writing was on the wall for these fine locos. Here, 'K3' Class 2-6-0 No. 61957 (built by NBL Co in 1935 and withdrawn from Colwick shed in September 1962) and BR Standard 'Britannia' Class 4-6-2 No. 70038 'Robin Hood' (built at Crewe in 1953, withdrawn from Carlisle Kingmoor in August 1967) are seen at rest inside Norwich shed.*

Colwick

◀ Introduced in 1911 by the Great Central Railway, the Class '04' 2-8-0 heavy freight loco went on to become the standard loco built for the Railway Operating Division (ROD) of the Royal Engineers during World War I. A total of 131 were built by the GCR, with an additional 521 being built for ROD. Of the latter 273 found their way on to the LNER's books during the 1920s. Even by May 2, 1965, with the end of steam on the ER in sight, Colwick shed was still allocated nine of these long-lived locos, including No. 63707 seen here.

This former Great Northern Railway shed was located on the main line to Grantham and Sleaford a few miles east of Nottingham. Its enormous allocation of freight locos reflected its importance in providing motive power for the heavy traffic from the Nottinghamshire coalfields. Colwick was recoded 16B when it came under LMR control only a few months prior to its closure to steam at the end of 1966.

The shed was about a 10-minute walk from Netherfield & Colwick station but its impregnable cordon made it virtually inaccessible to would-be trainspotters! By November 1961 Colwick's allocation had shrunk considerably to a total of 93 steam locos comprising 20 '04' 2-8-0s, 27 ex-WD 2-8-0s, 18 'B1' 4-6-0s, 15 'K3' 2-6-0s, 11 'L1' 2-6-4 tanks, one 'J50' and 2 'J94' 0-6-0 tanks and five ex-LMS Ivatt Class 4 2-6-0s.

▶ A shed bash to Derby, Colwick, Kirkby-in-Ashfield, Barrow Hill and Staveley (GC) was organised for September 7, 1965. However, the visit to Colwick was cut short by an irate shed foreman but not before ten locos had been seen, including two 'B1' 4-6-0s Nos. 61070 and 61141.

Staveley Barrow Hill

41 E

▼ By 1965 Barrow Hill had quite a collection of veteran steam locos - built in 1907, diminutive ex-MR Deeley 'OF' 0-4-0 tank No. 41528 was seen inside the roundhouse on 7 February 1965. A total of 10 of these locos were built for shunting in docks, breweries and industrial sites where their short wheelbase enabled them to traverse sharp curves. In addition to No. 41528, Barrow Hill was also allocated sister engine No. 41533 at this time and the remaining five of the veteran Johnson '1F' 0-6-0 half-cab tank locos introduced in 1878.

This former Midland Railway roundhouse was opened in 1870, but in 1958 came under the control of the Eastern Region and the shed's code was altered from 18D to 41E. Amongst the shed's allocation were ancient ex-Midland Railway tank locos used as shunters around the adjoining Staveley steel works. In late 1961 its allocation totalled 47 steam locos, including three of the diminutive ex-MR Deeley 'OF' 0-4-0 and seven of the ancient ex-MR Johnson '1F' 0-6-0 'half-cab' tanks, plus a selection of Ivatt Class 4 2-6-0s, Fowler '4F' 0-6-0s and Stanier '8F' 2-8-0s.

The shed was best reached either by taking a No. 99 bus from Sheffield or Chesterfield, or a 15-minute walk from Staveley Works station.

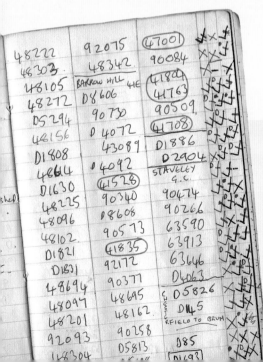

◄ Compared to Colwick, the visits to Kirkby-in-Ashfield and Barrow Hill sheds on September 7, 1965 were highly successful. Both sheds still housed many steam locos - of the 23 seen at Kirkby 19 were Stanier 8F 2-8-0s. Barrow Hill was still home to some ancient ex-MR locos used for working around the Staveley steel works, including Deeley 0-4-0 tank No. 41528 and Johnson half-cabs Nos. 41835, 41804, 41763 and 41708. To complete this spectacle was ex-LMS 0-4-0 saddle tank No. 47001.

Barrow Hill closed to steam in October 1965 and was then used as a diesel depot (recoded BH) for some years until the rundown and closure of the steel works. Fortunately, following closure in 1991, Barrow Hill was saved two days before it was due to be demolished and has since been preserved and reopened as a centre for the railway heritage movement.

Staveley GC

41 H

Opened by the Manchester, Sheffield & Lincolnshire Railway in 1892, Staveley (Great Central) was located on the east side of the Great Central main line a few minutes' walk from Staveley (Central) station. The shed's allocation in November 1961 was only 25 steam freight locos, of which 22 were ex-GCR Class '04' 2-8-0s – a reflection of the deliberate running down of freight services on the former GCR main line. Through freight services were totally withdrawn in June 1965 and the shed was closed. A quick trip to the desolate shed in September revealed the sorry sight of five stored locos, including two ex-WD 2-8-0s and three '04' 2-8-0s. The end came for the rest of the Great Central in September 1966.

▲ Taken on June 16, 1956, Gresley 'V2' Class 2-6-2 No. 60817 arrives at Staveley (Central) station on the Great Central main line. The grey, wet day makes the smoke cloud from the approaching engine particularly impressive. The trainspotter on the left takes up a gallant pose, eager to identify the emerging loco. The 'V2' was built at Darlington in 1937 and withdrawn from New England shed (34E) in June 1963.

◀ Class '04/7' 2-8-0 No. 63630 was one of 13 such Great Central workhorses still allocated to Staveley (GC) shed in May 1965. Closure came in June 1965.

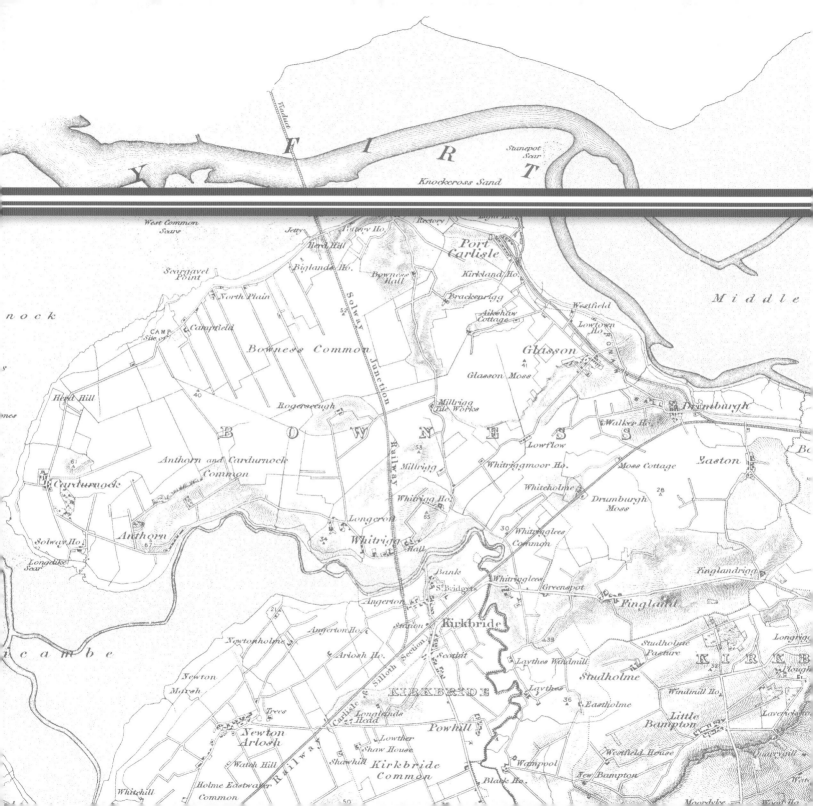

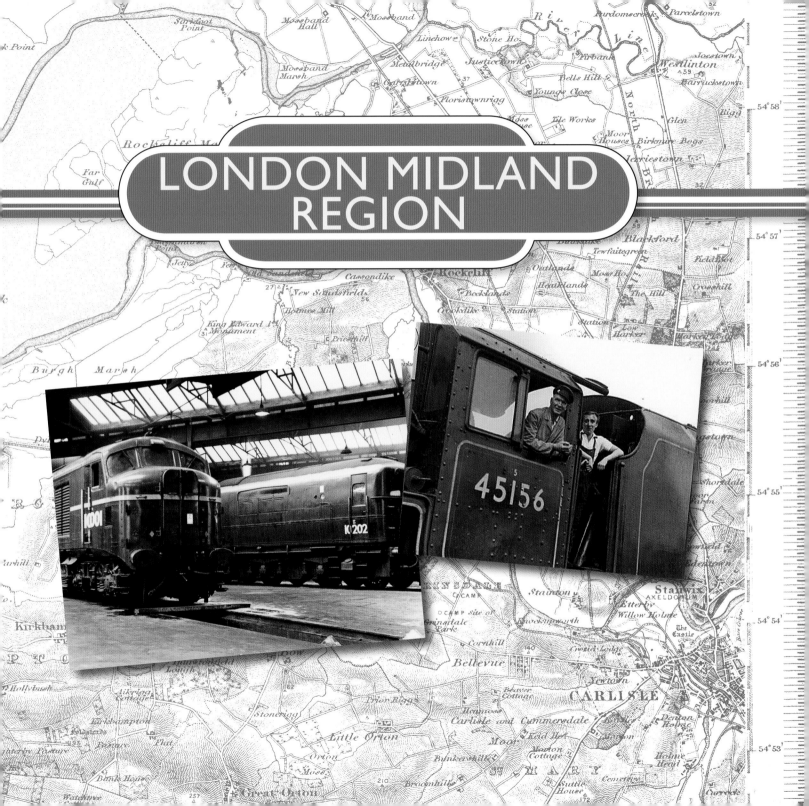

LONDON MIDLAND REGION

TOP SPOT

London Euston

Opened in 1837 as the London terminus of the London & Birmingham Railway, Euston station became the gateway for long-distance trains to the Midlands, northwest England and Scotland.

By the 1930s it also became the starting point for many famous express trains such as the 'Royal Scot' and the streamlined 'Coronation Scot', both destined for Glasgow. By the 1950s the list of romantically-named trains departing from Euston was impressive and included the 'Caledonian', the 'Emerald Isle Express', the 'Lakes Express', the 'Merseyside Express', the 'Midday Scot' and, of course, the 'Royal Scot'. At the same time Euston had become a great place for the locospotter to see LMR top link locos such as 'Jubilee', 'Royal Scot' and 'Patriot' 4-6-0s and the classic 'Princess' and 'Coronation' Class Pacifics.

Apart from the regular appearances of the two LMS Co-Co diesels (Nos 10000 and 10001) and the three SR main line diesels (Nos. 10201-10203), steam held sway until the introduction of the first English Electric Type 4 (Class 40) and BR Sulzer Type 4 (Class 44) diesels in 1960, but even their reign was short-lived with electrification of the West Coast Main Line proceeding apace, and by the early 1960s steam and diesel traction and Euston's days as a historic station building were all coming to an end. The station and its famous Euston Arch were demolished and, amidst much public outcry, replaced by the current modern bland building which opened in 1968. The end for diesels came so quickly that on a short visit to Euston in May 1966 only one was spotted – the rest were all 25kV AC electric locos. Now, even they are gone and tilting 'Pendolino' trains cover the journey to Glasgow in around 4½ hours.

▶ Then allocated to Willesden (1A) Stanier 'Black Five' 4-6-0 No. 44916 is seen here carrying out carriage shunting duties at Euston in April 1961. One of 842 such locos built between 1934 and 1951, No. 44916 was built at Crewe in 1945 and was withdrawn from Stockport Edgeley (9B) in December 1963.

▲ Stanier 'Coronation' Class 4-6-2 No. 46252 'City of Leicester', seen here at Euston in 1960, has just arrived with a train from the north. By that date the English Electric Type 4 (Class 40) diesels, seen on the right, were already usurping steam haulage on the WCML. Then allocated to Carlisle Kingmoor (12A), 'City of Leicester' was built at Crewe without streamlined casing (but with a streamlined tender) in 1944 and was withdrawn from Camden (1B) in June 1963.

▲ What Health & Safety? The carefully defaced notice invites intrepid trainspotters to venture beyond the platform at Euston as 'Black 5' 4-6-0 No. 45392 arrives with the 7.30am ex-Bletchley on 4 August 1960.

► A lone admirer gazes at 'Coronation' Class 4-6-2 No. 46236 'City of Bradford' as it waits to depart from Euston station with a down express in 1960.

SPECIAL NOTICE

ENGINE SPOTTERS

MUST NOT

PASS BEYOND

THIS BOARD

London Camden

The first engine shed at Camden, 1½ miles north of Euston station, was opened in 1837 to the east of the newly-built London & Birmingham Railway. At that time trains out of Euston were hauled uphill to Camden Town by cables until 1847 when more powerful steam locos were introduced. A new roundhouse was built on the site by the L&BR but, although closed in 1871, this famous building has been preserved and is now in use as an arts and concert venue. The Camden shed known and beloved by trainspotters – a five minute walk from Chalk Farm underground station – was opened on the west side of the main line in 1847 and modernised and enlarged in turn by both the L&NWR and the LMS. Under both companies it became the main shed for the top link West Coast Main Line Expresses from Euston and consequently had an allocation of locos that were definitely in the celebrity status! During the early BR era, Camden, with its allocation of Stanier 'Princess' and 'Coronation' Pacifics, supplied motive power for famous trains such as the 'Royal Scot' and 'The Caledonian'. 1960 saw the introduction of English Electric Type 4 (Class 40) and BR Sulzer

▲ *Despite being a top link shed, Camden also had a small allocation of 'Jinty' 0-6-0 tanks which were used on local duties. Here, on August 1, 1959 No. 47307 rubs shoulders with its main line shed mates including, on the far right, 'Royal Scot' Class 4-6-0 No. 46106 'Gordon Highlander'. The latter was unique in its class as it was fitted with BR style straight smoke deflectors. The 'Scot' was built by the NBL Co. in 1927, rebuilt in 1949 and withdrawn from Leicester Central (15E) in December 1962. However, due to the arctic winter conditions existing at that time it was reinstated until April 1963. No. 47307 was built by Hunslet in 1925 and withdrawn in August 1966.*

◄ *A visit to Camden was made during a 'shed bash' around London on September 4, 1962. Despite the high numbers of English Electric Type 4 seen on shed that day there were still five 'Coronation' Pacifics (Nos. 46227, 46240, 46239, 46236 and 46229) and one 'Princess Royal' Pacific (No. 46206) to be seen. The shed closed to steam a year later.*

Type 4 (Class 44) diesels on many of these services and by November 1961 Camden had lost all of its 'Royal Scot' and 'Jubilee' 4-6-0s and its 'Princess' Pacifics – all that was left were four 'Coronation' Pacifics and these were soon to go. At the same time, on the diesel side, the shed had 19 of the English Electric Type 4 diesels (including eight named members) and four of the early named 'Peak' (Class 44) diesels. Camden officially closed to steam in September 1963, but carried on as a diesel depot until 1966 when it succumbed to the electrification of the WCML and was finally closed.

▶ *This brass tally or pay token was issued to driver or fireman No. 52 of Camden shed by the London & North Western Railway.*

◀ Camden was justly famous for its allocation of 'Coronation' Pacifics, but by 1963 their days were numbered due to the increasing availability of Type 4 diesels. Here, on April 28, green-liveried No. 46239 'City of Chester' awaits transfer to Crewe North shed from where it was withdrawn in September 1964.

◀ Fitted with a red-background shedplate, 'Royal Scot' Class 4-6-0 No. 46156 'The South Wales Borderer' was seen on shed in April 1963 - only five months before Camden closed to steam. Built at Derby in 1930 the 'Scot' was rebuilt in 1954 and withdrawn from Annesley shed (16B) in October 1964. This loco should not be confused with ex-GWR 'Castle' Class 4-6-0 No. 4037 which carried a very similar name - 'The South Wales Borderers'.

London Willesden

▼ *Gavin Morrison captured this view inside Willesden's roundhouse on August 12, 1956. From left to right: WD 2-8-0 No. 90726 from Farnley Junction shed; 'Jubilee' 4-6-0 No. 45638 'Zanzibar'; unnamed and unrebuilt 'Patriot' 4-6-0 No. 45517.*

Originally opened by the L&NWR in 1873, Willesden depot went through various rebuildings and additions under the LMS until it ended up as a roundhouse and adjacent straight shed. The principal LMR shed for freight locos in London, by November 1961 its allocation was a very mixed bag that totalled 131 locos, of which 48 were diesels. Included in the latter were the two ex-LMS 1947/48-built Co-Co diesels and the three later Southern Region Ashford-built 1Co-Co1 diesels, 21 BR Sulzer Type 2 (Class 24), seven English Electric Type 2 (class 20) and 15 diesel shunters.

On the steam side 13 different classes were represented including two 'Princess Royal' Class Pacifics (relegated from 1B Camden), three rebuilt 'Patriot' and four 'Royal Scot' 4-6-0s, 21 Stanier 8F 2-8-0s, and five 'Britannia' Pacifics. Willesden shed was located on the west side of the main line out of Euston, just north of Willesden Junction station, from which it was just a five minute walk. A trainspotting visit to the shed in September 1962 ended with a tally of 33 diesels and 88 steam locos.

Following electrification of the West Coast Main Line the shed closed completely in August 1965.

▶ *Early diesel days at Willesden - seen here inside the roundhouse on May 9, 1962, ex-LMS main line diesel No. 10001 and ex-SR main line diesel No. 10102 were among the earliest diesels allocated to Willesden. The precursors to the first-generation diesels ordered in the 1955 Modernisation Plan, No. 10001 was withdrawn in 1962 and No. 10202 was withdrawn at the end of 1963.*

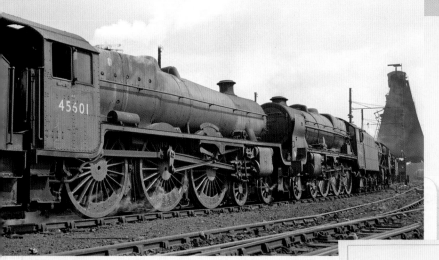

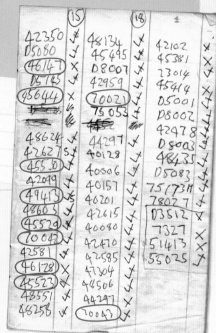

Also captured for posterity by Mike Esau at Willesden shed in 1962 are 'Jubilee' Class 4-6-0 No. 45601 'British Guiana' and 'Royal Scot' Class 4-6-0 No. 46125 '3rd Carabinier'.

By the afternoon of September 4, 1962 I arrived exhausted at Willesden shed. Seen here among a total of 33 diesels and 88 steam locomotives were 'Jubilee'' No. 45644, rebuilt 'Patriot' Nos. 45523, 45529 and 45530, 'Royal Scot' Nos. 46128 and 46147, 'Britannia' Nos. 70021, 70042 and 70043 and veteran ex-LNWR 'G2' Class 0-8-0 No. 49413.

'Coronation' Class 4-6-2 No. 46235 'City of Birmingham' of Crewe North was seen at Willesden in immaculate condition on May 11, 1963. It was built with a streamlined casing at Crewe in 1939, de-streamlined in 1946 and withdrawn from Crewe North (5A) in September 1964. It has since been preserved as a static exhibit in Birmingham.

Willesden-allocated rebuilt 'Patriot' class 4-6-0 No. 45530 'Sir Frank Ree' waits its next turn of duty on May 11, 1963. Built with a parallel-boiler at Crewe in 1930 this loco received its name after it was transferred from No. 5501 in 1937. Rebuilt with a taper boiler in 1947 it was withdrawn from Carlisle Kingmoor shed (12A) at the end of 1965.

TOP SPOT

London St Pancras

Designed by William Barlow, St Pancras station with its Victorian Gothic frontage and enormous cast iron train shed was opened in 1868 as the London terminus of the Midland Railway.

At the time of its opening the station was considered one of the wonders of the Victorian Age. Built on cast iron piers, the space below the station was used to store beer barrels carried by MR trains from Burton-upon-Trent. On the formation of the Big Four in 1923 the former L&NWR terminus at Euston was chosen by the newly-formed LMS as its main London terminus and St Pancras was then relegated to playing second fiddle with services for the Midlands and the North.

By Nationalisation the principal services from St Pancras continued to serve Nottingham, Manchester, Sheffield and Carlisle with named trains such as 'The Palatine' (to Manchester), 'The Waverley' (to Edinburgh via the Settle & Carlisle and Waverley routes) and the 'Thames-Clyde Express' (to Glasgow St Enoch via the Settle & Carlisle route and Dumfries). Prior to dieselisation in the early 1960s these trains were usually drawn by Kentish Town (14B) 'Jubilee' or 'Royal Scot' 4-6-0s. However, steam soon gave way to diesel in the shape of the 'Peak' Class (Class 45) of which some 16 had been allocated to Cricklewood diesel depot by November 1961 along with a number of BR Sulzer Type 2s (Class 24).

Between 1960 and 1966 'The Midland Pullman', operated by Blue Pullman diesel units, ran between St Pancras and Manchester Central. 'The Palatine' made its last run in 1964, 'The Waverley' ceased to run in 1968 when the line between Carlisle and Edinburgh via Hawick was closed and the 'Thames-Clyde Express' ended in 1975. HST sets took over remaining services to Leicester and Nottingham in 1983 and, since 2007, St Pancras has taken on a new lease of life as the London terminus of Eurostar services to Paris and Brussels.

▲ With two trainspotters lurking in the shadows, rebuilt 'Patriot' Class 4-6-0 No. 45532 'Illustrious' heads out from under the overall roof of St Pancras station with a northbound express, c.1960.

▼ One of five such locos then allocated to Kentish Town (14B) ex-LMS Fowler Class '4' 2-6-4 tank No. 42334 is seen on station pilot duties at St Pancras on February 28, 1962. A total of 125 of these locos were built at Derby between 1927 and 1934, the final 26 being fitted with side-window cabs. No. 42334 was built in 1929 and withdrawn from Trafford Park shed (9E) at the end of 1965.

◀ Allocated to Leeds Holbeck, ex-LMS 'Jubilee' Class 4-6-0 No. 45651 'Shovell' is here seen at St Pancras in January 1952 at the head of a train to Derby. A widely travelled engine, it was later transferred to Bristol (Barrow Road) shed (82E) until ending its days at Shrewsbury (89A) in 1961 where it often headed trains over the Central Wales Line to Swansea. It was built at Crewe in 1935 and withdrawn in November 1962.

▶ When rebuilt, the 'Royal Scot' 4-6-0s were fairly handsome engines. Allocated to Kentish Town (14B) and watched by two young trainspotters, No. 46133 'The Green Howards' waits to depart with the 5.25pm 'Robin Hood' restaurant car express to Nottingham in 1961. Built by the North British Locomotive Co. in 1927 and rebuilt in 1944, this loco was soon to move to Newton Heath (26A) from where it was withdrawn in February 1963.

Cricklewood

14 A

Consisting of two adjoining ex-Midland Railway roundhouses, the steam shed at Cricklewood was located on the west side of the main line about a 15 minute walk north of Cricklewood station and provided motive power for freight services on the Midland main line. With the opening of a diesel shed on the east side of the main line in 1960, Cricklewood's steam allocation was rapidly dwindling and by November 1961 totalled only 43 locos made up of six Ivatt Class 4 2-6-0s, eight Fowler 4F 0-6-0s, seven 'Black Five' 4-6-0s, six 'Jinty' 0-6-0 tanks and 16 Stanier 8F 2-8-0s. On the diesel shed by that date were 16 'Peak' Class (Class 45), 10 BR Sulzer Type 2 (Class 24) and 11 shunters. The steam shed closed in December 1964.

▼ A foreigner from Yorkshire visits Cricklewood - Gresley 'V2' 2-6-2 No. 60925 from York (50A) was seen on shed in October 1962. Note the Standard Eight parked by the shed entrance. Built at Darlington in 1941, the 'V2' spent most of its life allocated to 50A and was withdrawn from that shed in May 1964.

▼ A contrast in motive power at Cricklewood on October 21, 1962. 'Peak' Class diesel (Class 45) D123 stands next to rebuilt 'Patriot' class 4-6-0 No. 45532 'Illustrious'. The 'Peak' was built at Crewe in 1961, withdrawn as TOPS No. 45125 in May 1987 and has since been preserved. The 'Patriot' was built with a Fowler parallel boiler at Crewe in 1933, rebuilt in 1948 and withdrawn from Carlisle Upperby shed in February 1964.

▲ A visitor from Royston shed (55D) - the penultimate member of its class, BR Standard Class 5 4-6-0 No. 73170 was seen at Cricklewood on December 16, 1962. Built at Doncaster in 1957 this loco was only nine years old when withdrawn from Eastleigh (70D) in June 1966.

◄ A visitor from Leeds - ex-LMS 'Jubilee' Class 4-6-0 No. 45605 'Cyprus' from Holbeck shed (55A) receives an inspection at Cricklewood on May 11, 1963. Built by the North British Locomotive Co. in 1935, 'Cyprus' was withdrawn from Burton shed (16F) in February 1964.

Birmingham New Street

One of the busiest stations in the UK, the original subterranean New Street station was built jointly by the London & North Western Railway and the Midland Railway and opened in 1854.

Congestion soon led to the building of a separate adjacent station by the Midland Railway and this, along with major track improvements, was completed by 1885. Following severe damage to the station during World War II, the overall roof was removed in the early 1950s. However, despite New Street being one of the most depressing and grimy stations on the BR network, it still attracted its fair share of trainspotters during the 1950s and early '60s.

The obvious attraction was that the station served through services on two main lines – a loop of the West Coast Main Line and the ex-MR route from Derby to Bristol. Consequently they were treated to a wide range of ex-LMS and BR steam classes burrowing through the tunnels into the gloomy depths of the station on their journeys to the north and south. In addition to the 'Coronations' and 'Britannia' Pacifics and 'Jubilee', 'Patriot', 'Royal Scot', 'Black Five' and BR Standard Class 5 4-6-0s, the station was also alive with the comings and goings of the more humble 2P 4-4-0s on local trains to the south and on station pilot duty.

The early 1960s witnessed the arrival of the new English Electric Type 4 (Class 40) diesels on WCML duties and 'Peaks' (Class 45 and 46), newly-outshopped from Derby and Crewe, on the former Midland route. By 1964, with electrification of the WCML in progress, change was in the air for New Street. The old station was demolished and the current modern structure was opened in 1967. All services on the WCML were now in the hands of electric locos but, until the introduction of HST services, diesel locos continued to reign for some years on the Midland route.

▶ Immaculately restored, preserved ex-Midland Railway Compound 4-4-0 No. 1000 attracts many young admirers at New Street before departing with an SLS enthusiasts special to York and Doncaster on August 30, 1959.

▲ Despite its dingy surroundings, New Street attracted its fair share of trainspotters – BR Standard 'Britannia' Class 4-6-2 No. 70021 'Morning Star' attracts a group of admirers at New Street some time in the early 1960s. Built at Crewe in 1951, 'Morning Star' was withdrawn from Carlisle Kingmoor shed (12A) at the end of 1967.

◀ The driver and fireman of BR 'Britannia' Class 4-6-2 No. 70031 'Byron' exchange banter with a group of trainspotters at Birmingham New Street in 1960.

▶ On a trip to Birmingham on 6 September 1963 there was still plenty of steam and diesel activity at both Snow Hill and New Street stations – two 'Halls', a 'Modified Hall' and a 'Grange' were seen at the former while six 'Black 5s' and 'Jubilee No. 45617 'Mauritius' were seen at New Street.

▲ A group of drivers and firemen await their next turn of duty as ex-LMS 'Jubilee' Class 4-6-0 No. 45579 'Punjab' blows-off before departing from the cramped confines of New Street with a Pembroke Dock to Derby train on August 10, 1963. 'Punjab' was built by the North British Locomotive Co. in 1934 and withdrawn from Derby (16C) in August 1964.

◀ 'Black Five' 4-6-0 No. 45272 (built by Armstrong Whitworth in 1936 and withdrawn from Oxley shed in October 1965) attracts interest at New Street as it departs with a northbound train on August 10, 1963. The lad nearest to the camera appears rather bored – he's probably seen this Saltley (21A) loco hundreds of times before!

Saltley

21 A

▲ BR Standard Class 5 4-6-0 No. 73069 receives attention from the welder at Saltley on November 22, 1964. In the background, complete with yellow diagonal cabside warning sign, is withdrawn 'Jubilee' class 4-6-0 No. 45674 'Duncan' (minus nameplates) awaiting its fate at Draper's scrapyard in Hull.

Located a 10-minute walk south from Saltley station, Saltley shed was partially visible to the east of the ex-Midland Railway main line from Birmingham New Street to Derby. This large shed consisted of three adjoining roundhouse sheds, the earliest of which was opened by the MR in 1868. It was the most important Midland shed in Birmingham and supplied motive power for both freight and passenger duties on services south to Gloucester and Bristol and north to Derby and beyond. By the end of 1961, while being allocated 23 0-6-0 diesel shunters, the shed still had 140 steam locomotives on its books despite increasing dieselisation of passenger services on the main line between Derby and Bristol. By this time Saltley's allocation was a motley mix of 12 different classes of loco, ranging from 12 of the ancient ex-MR Johnson 3F 0-6-0s (soon to be scrapped), 35 4F 0-6-0s, 42 'Black Five', two rebuilt 'Patriot' and three 'Jubilee' 4-6-0s to nine Stanier 8F 2-8-0s and 13 BR 9F 2-10-0s. Saltley was recoded 2E in 1963 and finally closed to steam in March 1967.

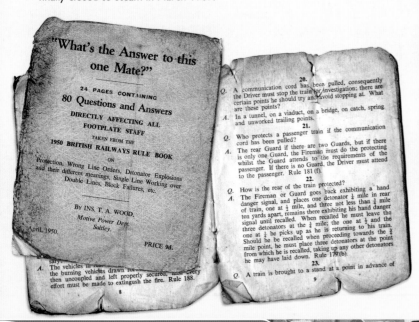

▲ Stanier 'Black Five' 4-6-0 No. 44691 and BR Standard '9F' 2-10-0 No. 92138 in Saltley's roundhouse in November 1964. The 'Black Five' was built at Horwich in 1950 and withdrawn from Workington shed (12D) in April 1967; the '9F' was built at Crewe in 1957 and was withdrawn from Speke Junction shed (8C) in July 1967.

◀ Giants at rest inside Saltley roundhouse on January 31, 1965 - from left to right: 'Black Five' 4-6-0 No. 45369 (built by Armstrong Whitworth in 1937, withdrawn from Chester (6A) in March 1967); BR Standard '9F' 2-10-0 No. 92125 (built at Crewe in 1957 and withdrawn from Carlisle Kingmoor (12A) at the end of 1967); ex-GWR 'Grange' Class 4-6-0 No. 6817 'Gwenddwr Grange' visiting from Worcester (built at Swindon in 1936 and withdrawn from Worcester (85A) in April 1965).

▶ Saltley was renowned for its large allocation of ancient ex-MR Johnson '3F' 0-6-0 freight locos. Over 900 of these locos were built for the Midland Railway between 1882 and 1908 and many lasted through to Nationalisation. Seven were also built in 1896 for the Somerset & Dorset Joint Railway. The final withdrawals took place in 1964 but none of this class has been preserved. A typical line-up is seen here at Saltley in 1955 - the foremost loco, No. 43374, was built in 1892 and was withdrawn in 1961.

◀ Despite closure to steam in 1967, Saltley continued to operate as a diesel depot. Here, Class 31 No. 31125 of Stratford shed was seen visiting Saltley on November 8, 1980. Built by Brush, these first-generation diesels were introduced between 1957 and 1962 and some have survived Privatisation into the 21st Century. 33 have been preserved.

▲ With an ear-splitting noise, stays are driven into a locomotive's firebox at Derby Works in the early 1950s.

DERBY HAD BECOME THE HEADQUARTERS of the Midland Railway on that company's formation in 1844 and all of its locomotive building was concentrated here. Under its Chief Mechanical Engineers Matthew Kirtley (1844–1873), Samuel Johnson (1873–1903), Richard Deeley (1903-1907) and Henry Fowler (1907–1922) Derby produced vast numbers of highly successful locomotive types ranging from the graceful 4-2-2 'Midland Spinners', the handsome 4-4-0 'Midland Compounds' and hundreds of rugged 0-6-0 freight locos – many of the latter class managed to continue in service until the early 1960s.

The Midland Railway had always had a small engine policy so that double-heading on heavily loaded trains was usually the order of the day. The only exceptions to this were the eleven 7F 2-8-0 freight locos built for the Somerset & Dorset Railway between 1914 and 1925 and the solitary 0-10-0, nicknamed 'Big Bertha', designed by James Clayton and built in 1919 for banking duties on the Lickey Incline. Despite this nothing much changed at Derby after the 1923 Big Four Grouping – 98 2P 4-4-0s and 70 2-6-2 tanks were turned out between 1928 and 1932 – until the final 20 of Fowler's 'Royal Scot' Class 4-6-0 which were built here in 1930.

Everything changed in 1932 when William Stanier was appointed CME. Under his big engine policy the majority of the LMS main line express locomotives were built at Crewe although Derby did build ten of his 'Jubilee' Class 4-6-0s and went on to build other Stanier locos including ten 0-4-4 tanks, 114 2-6-2 tanks, 113 4-cylinder 2-6-4 tanks, 37 3-cylinder 2-6-4 tanks and, during World War II, a large batch of 'Black Five' 4-6-0s.

After the War the Works was kept busy constructing 220 Fairburn 2-6-4 tanks, some of which were built after Nationalisation. In addition to building ten Ivatt push-pull fitted 2-6-2 tanks in 1952, Derby was heavily involved in the building of BR Standard locos including 130 of the highly successful Class 5 4-6-0 between 1951 and 1957, and 15 Class 4 2-6-4 tanks. In June 1957 Class 5 4-6-0 No. 73154 became the 2,941st and last steam loco to be built at Derby.

Derby was also involved in the building of Britain's first main line diesels including the Ivatt-designed LMS Co-Co locos Nos 10000 and 10001 (built 1947-48), the unique experimental Fell loco No. 10100 (built 1952) and a batch of the early (Class 11) diesel shunters. From 1958 to 1962 the Works went on to build a batch of the Class 08 diesel shunters, several batches of BR Sulzer Type 2 (Class 24/25), all ten of the early 'Peak' Class (Class 44 D1-D10), a batch of the later Class 45 Peaks and the full complement of Class 46 Peaks (D138-D193). Last but not least, Derby Carriage & Wagon Works in Litchurch Lane had turned out some of the first diesel multiple units to be made in Britain, including the famous 'Derby Lightweights' of 1953.

While Derby Works has now closed, production of passenger rolling stock including new sets for London Underground continues under private ownership at Litchurch Lane.

Derby Works

◀ Interior view of Derby Works Erecting Shop in the early 1950s showing a line up headed by two ex Midland Railway stalwarts in the form of Class 3F 'Jinty' 0-6-0T No. 47249 and Class 4F 0-6-0 No. 43887, both undergoing a general overhaul.

▶ A notebook from a visit to Derby Works in June 1962. It was busy on the last batch of BR Sulzer Type 4 (Class 46) main line diesels.

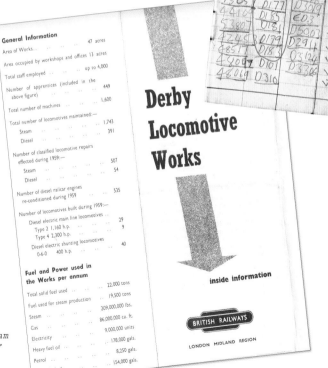

▲ Then allocated to Stafford (5C), Fowler 2-6-4 tank No. 42347 undergoes a major overhaul at its birthplace in the early 1950s. Built in 1929, this loco was withdrawn from Barrow shed (12E) in September 1962.

▶ Visitors to Derby Works in the early 1960s were handed a useful information leaflet. Apparently Derby repaired 507 steam and 54 diesel locos during 1959. The Works also built 9 'Peak' Class Type 4 diesels and 29 Type 2 diesels during that year.

General Information

Area of Works	47 acres
Area occupied by workshops and offices	13 acres
Total staff employed	up to 4,000
Number of apprentices (included in the above figure)	449
Total number of machines	1,600
Total number of locomotives maintained:—	1,743
Steam	
Diesel	391
Number of classified locomotive repairs effected during 1959:—	
Steam	507
Diesel	54
Number of diesel railcar engines re-conditioned during 1959	535
Number of locomotives built during 1959:—	
Diesel electric main line locomotives	
Type 2 1,160 h.p.	29
Type 4 2,300 h.p.	9
Diesel electric shunting locomotives 0-6-0 400 h.p.	40

Fuel and Power used in the Works per annum

Total solid fuel used	22,000 tons
Fuel used for steam production	19,500 tons
Steam	209,000,000 lbs.
Gas	86,000,000 cu. ft.
Electricity	9,000,000 units
Heavy fuel oil	178,000 gals.
Petrol	8,250 gals.
Diesel fuel oil	154,000 gals.

Derby
Locomotive
Works

inside information

BRITISH RAILWAYS

LONDON MIDLAND REGION

Derby

17 A

▲ Derby in 1953 with ubiquitous '8F' 2-8-0 No. 48138 in the centre and ex-LMS 'Crab' 2-6-0 No. 42872 - a Crewe engine - in the background and carrying a 'Special' reporting number. These highly capable and adaptable Moguls were used extensively on specials, both passenger and freight. 245 members of the class were built and allocated to depots nationwide. They could be seen in many parts of Britain and, as such, represented a great challenge to trainspotters.

The Midland Railway was the first large scale amalgamation of several small railway concerns into one larger company. The earliest engine shed at Derby, centre of the new company's operations from 1844, had been opened by the Midland Counties Railway in 1839 and the final double roundhouse shed was opened in 1890 by the Midland itself.

Located at the south side of Derby Midland station to the east of the main line to St Pancras it was a popular destination for trainspotters who were usually able to take in a tour of both the shed and adjacent works.

Once home to the elegant '4P' Compound and '2P' 4-4-0s, by late 1961, with brand new 'Peaks' emerging from the neighbouring Works and the dieselisation of the Midland lines, the shed's steam allocation had fallen to 65 with 11 different classes represented. The seven 'Jubilee' and six BR standard Class 5 4-6-0s had pride of place but there were still some home grown vintage characters around, including four ex-MR Johnson 3F 0-6-0s (dating from 1885) and three ex-MR Johnson 3F 0-6-0 tanks (built in 1899).

On the diesel side the invasion had well and truly begun and by late 1961 Derby shed had an allocation of no less that 50 'Peaks' (class 45/46) which had recently arrived shining and new from the adjacent Works.

At the same time Derby had been allocated the entire class (D5700-D5719) of the unreliable Co-Bo 'Metrovick' (Class 28) diesels which had been introduced in 1958 and had been returned to their manufacturers, Metropolitan-Vickers, for urgent remedial work. Originally used on the 'Condor' express freight service, for their sins, they all finally ended up in Barrow-in-Furness (12E) and were withdrawn by 1969.

From 1963 until closure to steam in Spring 1967, when it was replaced by a diesel maintenance depot, Derby shed carried the code of 16C. Derby's only sub-shed was at the former Great Northern Railway terminus station of Friargate. This was closed in 1955.

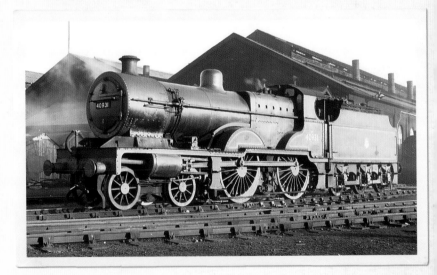

▲ Ex-LMS '4P' Compound 4-4-0 No. 40931 is seen here at Derby, presumably ex works, in 1953. Far away from its natural haunts, being allocated to Llandudno Junction (6G), the loco used to work stopping passenger trains along the North Wales Main Line. Built at the Vulcan Foundry in 1927 this loco was withdrawn in October 1958.

▲ A foreign visitor to Derby in September 1956 was ex-GER 'D16' Class 4-4-0 No. 62564 which had just completed a turn from Lincoln via Nottingham. Built at Stratford Works in 1908 this elegant Edwardian machine was withdrawn from Lincoln (40A) in March 1958. Behind it Fowler 2-6-4 tank No. 42358 has just emerged from the neighbouring works in a fresh coat of paint.

▶ 'Peak' Class diesel (Class 45) D82, at Derby during a visit in the early '60s, was withdrawn as TOPS No. 45141 in August 1988.

Toton

Stapleford and Sandiacre

18 A

▶ Home to many of the ex-LMS Beyer Garratt 2-6-0+0-6-2 articulated locos, Toton shed was at the centre of heavy freight activities in the Nottinghamshire coalfield. Here, ex-MR Deeley '3F' 0-6-0 No. 43798 and Beyer Garratt No. 47969 stand under the coaling tower in the mid-1950s.

▼ After closure to steam, Toton continued to be a magnet for trainspotters with its wide variety of diesel types. Here a pair of Class 20 locos, 20077 and 20071, pass Toton Sidings on June 7, 1975 with a southbound train of cement 'Presflos'.

Located midway between Derby and Nottingham, Toton motive power depot was the principal freight engine shed in the heart of the Derby/Nottingham coalfield and supplied motive power for shunting and freight trains at the adjacent marshalling yard.

By the early 1950s Toton Marshalling Yard was one of the busiest and largest mechanised marshalling yards in Europe and was capable of handling over 3,000 wagonloads each day. Although not a glamorous destination for the trainspotter, Toton – especially on a Sunday – could yield vast numbers of freight locos to cross off in the ABC book.

It was located on the west side of the former Midland main line between Long Eaton and Stapleford & Sandiacre stations, being about a 15-minute walk from the latter. There had been a shed at Toton since the Midland Railway opened one here in the mid-19th century but with later alterations and additions by both the MR and BR the depot had grown to three adjacent roundhouses by 1948. Many of the ex-LMS Beyer Garratt 2-6-0+0-6-2 articulated locos – first introduced in 1927 – were also stationed at Toton to haul heavy coal trains. Numbered by BR 47967–47999, the 33 members of this class were withdrawn over the period between 1955 and 1958.

Apart from the addition of 12 diesel shunters used in the adjoining marshalling yard, Toton was still an all-steam shed even in November 1961 with an allocation of 86 locos. This not only included 52 Stanier 8F 2-8-0s,

13 BR Standard 9F 2-10-0s and 16 4F 0-6-0s but also an ancient Johnson 3F 0-6-0 tank and two Johnson 2F 0-6-0s. The latter were soon to go to the great scrapyard in the sky, but Toton clung on until the end of 1965 when it closed to steam. It retained its importance with a 16-road diesel depot and was later a major centre for spotting many diesel classes including 20, 31, 37, 44, 45. 46, 47, 56, 58 and, more recently, 60 and 66.

Toton is still used today for the heavy maintenance of EWS diesel locos.

▶ Seen here at Toton in September 1958, ex-LMS Class '3F' 'Jinty' 0-6-0 tank No. 47551 was built by Hunslet Engineering in 1928 and spent many years shunting at Toton. It was withdrawn in February 1963. On the right is ex-London, Tilbury & Southend Railway 4-4-2 tank No. 41947 which was built at Derby in 1927 and was usually seen at work on the Fenchurch Street to Tilbury and Southend lines. No. 41947 eventually found its way to Toton and, as the last member of its class, was withdrawn at the end of 1960. No. 41966 is preserved as LTSR No. 80 'Thundersley'.

Manchester

▲ Pure nostalgia – this wonderfully detailed photo taken at London Road station in 1960 surely sums up the joy of trainspotting. With electrification gathering pace in the background and watched by an excited group of spotters, red-liveried 'Coronation' Class 4-6-2 No. 46243 'City of Lancaster' (built Crewe 1940, withdrawn from Edge Hill (8A) in September 1964) enters the station with an express from Euston. Beyond the LNWR signals and water tower, English Electric Type 4 (Class 40) D220 (built 1959, named 'Franconia' in 1963 and withdrawn in 1982) waits to depart with an up express.

Apart from London, Manchester and its suburbs in the late 1950s and early '60s probably boasted more attractions for trainspotters than anywhere else in the UK. It not only had four major railway stations but seven engine sheds and two railway works.

Manchester London Road (now Piccadilly)

The station, opened in 1842 by the Manchester & Birmingham Railway, was considerably enlarged by the L&NWR and also used as the terminus of the Great Central Railway line from Sheffield. The latter route via Woodhead Tunnel and Penistone was electrified at 1,500V DC in 1954 and, until closure in 1970, brought EM1 (Class 76) and EM2 (Class 77) electric locos (based at 9C Reddish) into one side of London Road station. The rest of the station served main line services to the south via the West Coast Main Line to London Euston, including named trains such as 'The Lancastrian', 'The Comet' and 'The Mancunian'. Prior to electrification of this route in the early 1960s motive power for these trains was supplied by Longsight (9A) shed's allocation of 'Jubilee' and 'Royal Scot' 4-6-0s and 'Britannia' Pacifics. A short diesel interregnum saw the early named English Electric Type 4s (Class 40) only to be followed shortly by Class 83 25kv electric locos. To coincide with the electrification of the WCML, London Road station was rebuilt and renamed Piccadilly in 1960.

Manchester Victoria and Exchange

Originally opened in 1844 by the Manchester & Leeds Railway, Victoria station was considerably enlarged by the Lancashire & Yorkshire Railway in 1909. A through platform at the adjacent Exchange station (opened by the L&NWR in 1884, closed 1969) was linked to one of Victoria's platforms making it the longest in Europe. Destinations from Victoria ranged across the wide spectrum of former L&Y routes from Liverpool

▶ Thought to be Mr C W Thorp, the driver and his fireman of 'Black Five' 4-6-0 No. 45156 'Ayrshire Yeomanry' ponder their future on BR less than two months before the end of steam. Seen here as Manchester Victoria station pilot on June 15, 1968 this loco was built by Armstrong Whitworth in 1935 and withdrawn from Rose Grove shed (10F) in August.

▲ The last working 'Britannia' 4-6-2 No. 70013 'Oliver Cromwell' was in great demand to haul specials during the summer of 1968. Admired by two young enthusiasts and complete with its original home shed plate of 32A but with a painted name, it is seen passing westbound through Manchester Victoria station on June 10.

and Southport in the west to Huddersfield, Leeds, York, Goole and Hull in the east. Motive power for many of these trains came from Newton Heath shed (26A) which, in the 1950s and early '60s would have supplied 'Black Fives', 'Jubilees' or the occasional 'Patriot'. In the summer of 1968, it was still common to see 'Black Fives' or the occasional BR Standard Class 5 at work in the station on pilot duties, empty coaching stock or parcels trains – making Victoria one of the last city centre stations in the UK to see steam operations.

Manchester Central

Opened by the Cheshire Lines Committee in 1880, Central station was crowned with an enormous wrought–iron single span arched roof which can still be seen, in a different guise, today. It was used by the Midland Railway, and later the LMS, as its Manchester terminus for services to London St Pancras via Derby. Until 1964 the main express of the day was 'The Palatine' which ran to St Pancras via Millers Dale, Matlock, Derby and Leicester and until the introduction of the 'Peak' diesels was usually hauled by a 'Royal Scot', 'Jubilee' or 'Britannia'. A diesel Blue Pullman service from Central to St Pancras was introduced in July 1960 but was withdrawn in March 1967 following completion of the electrification of the WCML between Manchester and London Euston. Central station was closed in 1969 but has since been converted into a conference centre.

◄ Bereft of nameplate and with yellow cabside diagonal warning sign, ex-LMS 'Jubilee' Class 4-6-0 No. 45705 'Seahorse', allocated to Newton Heath (9D), waits to depart from a litter-strewn Manchester Central station with the 17.22 train to Buxton on June 29, 1965. Built at Crewe in 1936, 'Seahorse' was withdrawn from Newton Heath shed in November 1965.

Newton Heath

26A

Opened by the Lancashire & Yorkshire Railway in 1876, Newton Heath was a large 24-road engine shed that serviced steam locos for freight duties on former L&Y routes and passenger services operating out of Manchester's Victoria station until the last few months of steam on BR.

Altered by the LMS in the 1930s, Newton Heath was reduced in size in the late 1950s to make way for a new diesel depot. Located in the fork of the Miles Platting to Dean Lane, and Miles Platting to Newton Heath lines, the shed was quickly accessed on foot from either Newton Heath or Dean Lane stations.

Despite the reduction in its size and the onset of dieselisation the shed still had an allocation of 119 steam locos in November 1961. This comprised 15 different classes and included 30 'Black Five' (including two of the four named engines of this class, 45154 and 45156), one unrebuilt 'Patriot', one rebuilt 'Patriot', 11 'Jubilee' and four 'Royal Scot' 4-6-0s, 12 2-6-4 tanks, 11 'Crab' 2-6-0s, 20 ex-WD 2-8-0s and six BR 9F 2-10-0s.

The shed's code was changed to 9D in 1963 and it was closed to steam in 1968.

▲ *The famous ex L&YR Newton Heath Locomotive Shed on the Oldham Road, from where Manchester United football club began, was a true place of legend. Steam traction survived there almost until the end as witnessed in this scene featuring a Stanier '8F' 2-8-0 and two 'Black Five' 4-6-0 (Nos 45134 and 45312) in a grimy rundown condition in 1967.*

▶ *In August 1968, 'Black 5' 4-6-0 No. 45025 was seen in action at Newton Heath moving a 'dead' 'Black Five' around the yard. It is now one of 18 such locos preserved and is currently awaiting overhaul at Aviemore on the Strathspey Railway.*

◀ Along with 'Black Five' 4-6-0s, Stanier '8F' 2-8-0 No. 48356 was one of many ex-LMS locos standing silent inside Newton Heath shed in June 1968. By that date their only future trip would be to the breaker's yard.

▲ By 1968 Newton Heath was one of the last steam sheds still operating on BR. This photo taken from the footplate of 'Black Five' 4-6-0 No. 45096 on June 8, shows the shed yard in terminal decline. Built at Vulcan Foundry in 1935 the 'Black Five' only had two months more active service until being withdrawn from Rose Grove shed (10F) in August.

◀ Allocated to Carnforth (10A), 'Black Five' 4-6-0 No. 45025 was seen on Newton Heath's turntable in 1968. Built at Vulcan Foundry in 1934, this loco was withdrawn from Carnforth in August of that year.

Liverpool

The first Liverpool terminus of the Liverpool & Manchester Railway was located at Edge Hill in 1830. The line was later extended through a tunnel and down an incline to a new station at Lime Street which opened in 1836.

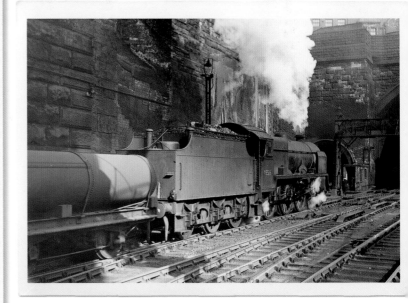

Before the onset of diesels (in the shape of English Electric Type 4s) on long-distance trains and the creeping WCML electrification (to Crewe in 1959 and to Euston in 1966), Lime Street offered a good choice of glamorous steam locos for the spotter. The station had its fair share of named trains to London including 'The Red Rose', 'The Merseyside Express', 'The Shamrock' and 'The Manxman'. Many of the locos for these trains came from Liverpool's main steam shed at Edge Hill (8A) and on a good day would include examples of 'Patriot', 'Jubilee' and 'Royal Scot 4-6-0s and 'Princess Royal' and 'Coronation' Pacifics. However, with the influx of 14 of the English Electric Type 4s, by November 1961 Edge Hill's steam allocation was down to 95 locos of which 34 were 'Black Five', seven unrebuilt 'Patriot', two rebuilt 'Patriot' and five 'Royal Scot' 4-6-0s along with one 'Princess' and four 'Coronation' Pacifics. Interestingly, Edge Hill was also home to one of the Fowler 2F 0-6-0 dock tanks and 16 of the ex-L&NWR 0-8-0 heavy freight locos. The shed finally closed to steam in May 1968 and the diesel depot closed in 1986.

The other major stations in Liverpool were Central and Exchange. Central was opened in 1874 by the Cheshire Lines Committee and provided services to Manchester Central, London St Pancras, Hull and Harwich. In 1966 most of its services were diverted to Lime Street and it was finally closed in 1972. Liverpool Central Low Level station was opened by the Mersey Railway in 1892 and the site is now used by Merseyrail Northern Line trains.

Exchange station became the Liverpool terminus of the Lancashire & Yorkshire Railway in 1886 and provided services to Manchester Victoria, Blackpool, Cumbria and Glasgow. It became the last city termini in the UK to see regular steam-hauled trains until the very end of steam on BR in August 1968. It closed in 1977.

▲ Looking extremely handsome and carrying the original British Railways motif on its tender, Edge Hill (8A) rebuilt 'Patriot' Class 4-6-0 No. 45527 'Southport' receives last minute attention before departing from Lime Street with an express for Newcastle in the early 1950s. 'Southport' was built at Derby in 1933, rebuilt in 1948 and withdrawn from Carlisle Kingmoor (12A) shed in December 1964.

◄ Unrebuilt 'Patriot' Class 4-6-0 No. 45516 'The Bedfordshire and Hertfordshire Regiment' fills in time with odd jobs while acting as standby engine at Lime Street on March 31, 1956. Carrying the largest nameplate of its class, No. 45516 was built at Crewe in 1932 and withdrawn from Warrington Dallam (8B) in August 1961.

▶ Modern traction at Lime Street – BR-built E3092 waits to depart with the up 'Manxman' to Euston in June 1964. The last part of the train's journey south would have been diesel-hauled as electrification through to Euston hadn't been completed by this date. E3092 was one of 40 'AL5' Bo-Bo main line electric locos built at Doncaster between 1961 and 1964. Later classified Class 85, this loco was withdrawn as No. 85037 in 1990.

◄ The very last day – to mark the end of steam haulage on British Railways a fair number of special trains were run in 1968. However, the very last train was the famous '15 Guinea Special' of August 11. The route taken was from Liverpool Lime Street, Manchester Victoria and over the Settle & Carlisle to Carlisle and return and was hauled at various stages by 'Black Five' 4-6-0s Nos. 44781, 44871 and 45110 and 'Britannia' Class Pacific No. 70013 'Oliver Cromwell'. Here, watched by a throng of enthusiasts and a couple of British Transport policemen, the train is seen waiting to depart from Lime Street at 9.10am on the first leg of its journey to Manchester Victoria behind 'Black Five' 4-6-0 No. 45110. This famous loco was built at the Vulcan foundry in 1935 and was withdrawn from Lostock Hall shed (10D) after hauling the special but has since been preserved.

Crewe

One of Britain's major railway junctions, Crewe station was opened in 1837 by the Grand Junction Railway. Its importance steadily grew, especially when the Grand Junction moved its locomotive works from Edge Hill to Crewe in 1843.

Two years later the London & North Western Railway was formed by the merger of the Grand Junction with the London & Birmingham Railway and Liverpool & Manchester Railway and Crewe Works grew from strength to strength. So did Crewe station and by the 1890s it had reached the limits of its capacity necessitating the building of a deviation line for through freight traffic.

With its major railway works and two large engine sheds Crewe retained its importance under the LMS and, later, in BR days. These attractions together with a multitude of services not only on the West Coast Main Line, but also to Manchester, Liverpool, Chester and North Wales, Shrewsbury and the Potteries brought trainspotters to bustling Crewe station in their droves. Even with the onset of WCML electrification in 1959, steam locos still could be seen in large numbers for a few more years.

By 1960, the diesel invasion had started and many of the WCML expresses were soon in the hands of English Electric Type 4 (Class 40) diesels, displacing the Stanier 'Princess Royal' and 'Coronation' Pacifics. In their twilight years these magnificent machines, along with the remaining 'Royal Scots' and 'Jubilees', were adorned with diagonal yellow stripes on the side of their cabs denoting that they weren't allowed to work 'under the wires' south of Crewe. Crewe North (5A) had closed by 1965 and the end came for steam in November 1967 when Crewe South (5B) was closed. Electrification proceeded apace until 1974 when the entire route from Euston to Glasgow was completed.

► Despite the creeping electrification of the WCML, Crewe still managed to retain its magic for trainspotters in the early 60s. Oblivious to the new electric loco on the next platform, this trainspotter gives his undivided attention to 'Royal Scot' Class 4-6-0 No. 46154 'The Hussar'. Built at Derby in 1930 and rebuilt in 1948, this loco was withdrawn from Willesden (1A) in November 1962.

▲ Pre-electrification days at Crewe – the usual gaggle of trainspotters at the north end of the station watch rebuilt 'Patriot' Class 4-6-0 No. 45522 'Prestatyn' arrive with a Llandudno to Euston train on July 20, 1957. Built at Derby in 1933 and rebuilt in 1949, 'Prestatyn' was withdrawn from Longsight shed (9A) in September 1964.

◀ Catching a few admiring glances, Edge Hill (8A) 'Princess Royal' Class 4-6-2 No. 46204 'Princess Louise' waits to depart from Crewe on November 25, 1960. Built at Crewe in 1935, this loco was one of the first four of its class to be withdrawn in October 1961.

▲ Under the wires – 'Royal Scot' Class 4-6-0 No. 46121 'Highland Light Infantry, City of Glasgow Regiment' of Polmadie shed (66A) at the head of a train from Glasgow on November 25, 1960. Bearing one of the two longest names of any 'Royal Scot' (the other was No. 46137 'The Prince of Wales's Volunteers (South Lancashire)') No. 46121 was built by the North British Locomotive Co in 1927, rebuilt in 1946 and withdrawn from Polmadie shed at the end of 1962.

◀ Ex-LMS prototype main line diesel No. 10000 and 'Coronation' Class 4-6-2 No. 46251 'City of Nottingham' meet under the wires at Crewe c.1960. Built at Derby in 1947 No. 10000 was withdrawn from Willesden shed (1A) in 1962. Built at Crewe without streamlined casing in 1944, No. 46251 had a slightly longer life and was withdrawn from Crewe North shed (5A) in October 1964.

Together with its important junction station and two major steam sheds, Crewe Works had to be one of the 'must visit' rail centres for trainspotters in the 1950s and early '60s.

▲ *Outside the main erecting shop at Crewe Works on 22 February 1959 after their last heavy general repair are 'Royal Scot' 4-6-0 No. 46145 'The Duke of Wellington's Regiment (West Riding)' and 'Super D' Class 0-8-0 No. 49246.*

BUILT BY THE GRAND JUNCTION RAILWAY on a green field site in 1843, Crewe Works grew to be the largest railway works in the UK. Within three years the merger of the GJR with the London & Birmingham and the Manchester & Birmingham Railways created the London & North Western Railway.

The LNWR eventually concentrated all of its loco building at Crewe and under its Chief Mechanical Engineers (John Ramsbottom 1857-1871; Francis Webb 1871–1903; George Whale 1903–1909; Charles Bowen-Cooke 1909–1920; H. P. M. Beames 1920–1922 and George Hughes 1922) produced over 6,000 new and rebuilt locos by the time of the Big Four Grouping in 1923.

Under the LMS Crewe went on to build 175 of Hughes' 2-6-0 'Crabs' and, from 1932, under its new CME William Stanier, went on to build some of the most successful steam locos in the UK. These included 25 2-6-2 tanks, 40 Moguls, a large batch of the 8F 2-8-0s, 142 Class 5 ('Black Five') 4-6-0s and 131 'Jubilee' 4-6-0s. By far the most famous of Stanier's locos built at Crewe were the 13 'Princess Royal' and 38 'Princess Coronation' Class Pacifics. These were followed by 65 of Ivatt's Class 2 2-6-0s and 120 of his 2-6-2 tanks – construction of both these classes started under the LMS but continued in production under BR until 1953.

Under BR Crewe Works went from strength to strength and went on to produce 55 Class 7 'Britannia' Pacifics between 1951 and 1954, ten Class 6 'Clan' Pacifics in 1952 and the unique Class 8 No. 71000 'Duke of Gloucester' Pacific in 1954. The final batch of steam locomotives built at Crewe were 198 of the Standard Class 9F 2-10-0s built between 1954 and 1958.

◀ *Heavy overhauls in the last years of steam as 'Britannia' 4-6-2 No. 70022 'Tornado' is seen here in the famous erecting shop at Crewe Works in the early 1960s. Little could it be imagined at that time that this loco's name would be bestowed on a new 'A1' Pacific half a century later. Built at Crewe in 1951, No. 70022 spent the 1950s on the WR before moving to the LMR where it was withdrawn from Carlisle Kingmoor shed (12A) at the end of 1967.*

Crewe Works

◀ Crewe Works built 198 BR Standard Class '9F' 2-10-0s between 1954 and 1958. Here, two examples await being reunited with their tenders after receiving overhaul at Crewe in February 1961. In 1958 No. 92250 became the 7,331st and last steam engine to be built at Crewe.

▼ Despite the end of steam on BR in 1968 Crewe Works continued to overhaul diesel locos for many more years. Seen undergoing overhaul inside the erecting shop on Open Day on September 18, 1971 were Class 50s Nos. 416 and 442 and Class 47 No. 1864.

◀ Between 1962 and early 1964, Crewe Works built 44 'Western' Class diesel hydraulic locos (D1030-D1073) for the Western Region. On a visit to the works in August 1962, D1037-D1051 were seen in various stages of construction, while D1036 was receiving last minute attention before delivery. The first of these handsome locos be built at Crewe was D1035, which had rolled out the month previously. The building of D1030-D1034 was switched from Swindon to Crewe, and consequently these five locos were the last to be built.

The Works went on to build large numbers of diesel locos: a batch of the numerous Class 08 diesel shunters, a batch of the BR Sulzer Type 2 (Class 24 and 25), the two power-cars of the prototype HST, 197 HST (Class 43) power-cars, a batch of the 'Peak' (Class 45), 202 Brush Type 4 (Class 47), 39 'Western' (Class 52) diesel-hydraulics for the Western Region and 20 Class 56. Crewe also built 36 Class 87 25kV AC electric locos for the West Coast Main Line, the prototype Class 89 No. 89001 'Avocet', 50 Class 90 and 31 Class 91 electric locos. By 1990 over 8,000 locos (steam, diesel and electric) had been built at Crewe. Now nothing much remains of what was once an industry that, at its peak, employed over 20,000 people.

Crewe North

5·A

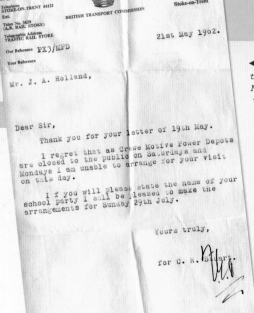

District Manager
C. R. STUART
Telephone
STOKE-ON-TRENT 44121
Ext.
Telex No. 3629
A. R. RAIL STOKE
Telegraphic Address
TRAFFIC RAIL STOKE
Our Reference PX3/MPD
Your Reference

District Manager
London Midland Region
British Railways
Stoke-on-Trent

BRITISH TRANSPORT COMMISSION

21st May 1962.

Mr. J. A. Holland,

Dear Sir,

Thank you for your letter of 19th May.

I regret that as Crewe Motive Power Depots are closed to the public on Saturdays and Mondays I am unable to arrange for your visit on this day.

If you will please state the name of your school party I shall be pleased to make the arrangements for Sunday 29th July.

Yours truly,

for C. R. Stuart.

◄ Well it was worth a try! Apparently Crewe North shed was closed to the public on Saturdays and Mondays. Sunday was always the best day to visit any shed as nearly all of its locos would be present but the only downside to this was that Sunday train services were extremely restricted. The Sabbath was still treated fairly seriously even in the early 1960s.

Up until 1965 Crewe had two very large loco sheds – Crewe North (5A) supplied locos primarily for main line passenger duties and Crewe South (5B) supplied locos mainly for freight and shunting duties. Crewe North, reached by a footbridge from the north of Platform 1 of Crewe station, was located to the west of the main line to the north of the station. An alternative route was a five-minute walk from the station via an alleyway and Station Street.

The shed was fairly modern having been built as a half roundhouse as recently as 1950 and its allocation during the '50s included many top link locos for service on the West Coast Main Line, including Stanier 'Princess' and 'Coronation' Pacifics – all of them built in the 1930s at the nearby Crewe Works.

Despite creeping electrification and the diesel interregnum, the shed's allocation in November 1961 was still fairly impressive with a total of 96 steam locos and 30 diesels. Apart from a few Ivatt Class 2-6-2 and Stanier Class 4 2-6-4 tanks, all of the steam locos were definitely for main line duties and included 45 Stanier 'Black Five', 22 'Jubilee' and nine 'Royal Scot' 4-6-0s, one 'Princess Royal' and seven 'Coronation' Pacifics and the unique No. 71000 'Duke of Gloucester' Pacific. The entire diesel allocation was made up of three of the original named 'Peaks' (Class 44) and 27 English Electric Type 4 (Class 40).

Crewe North was closed in May 1965 but Crewe South lingered on until November 1967.

▼ Crewe North in the 1950s, and amongst the miscellany of motive power gathered beneath the coaling towers is 'Jubilee' Class 4-6-0 No. 45586 'Mysore' (built by NBL in 1934, withdrawn from Crewe South (5B) in January 1965), Fairburn 2-6-4 tank No. 42121 (built at Derby in 1949 and withdrawn from Birkenhead (8H) in July 1966) and Stanier 'Black Five' No. 45300 (built by Armstrong Whitworth in 1937 and withdrawn from Holyhead (6J) at the end of 1965).

▶ In April 1960 Crewe North only possessed one 'Britannia' but by April 1965 there were no less than 28 that had returned back to their birthplace. Many of these had found their way from Norwich via March after dieselisation in East Anglia. However, No. 70018 'Flying Dutchman', seen here at Crewe North, was one of several that had originally been allocated to Cardiff Canton (86C) for working expresses to Paddington. After a move to Carlisle Canal (12C) the 'Brit' ended up at 5A where it was seen on March 24, 1963. It was withdrawn from its final shed, Carlisle Kingmoor (12A), at the end of 1966.

◀ A view from inside Crewe North's semi-roundhouse in the early 1960s. In the foreground is 'Coronation' class 4-6-2 No 46256 'Sir William A. Stanier F.R.S.' and an unidentified 'Black Five'. On the 70ft turntable is 'Coronation' Class 4-6-2 No. 46232 'Duchess of Montrose'. The latter was withdrawn from Polmadie shed (66A) at the end of 1962 but 'Sir William' lasted nearly two more years until withdrawn from Crewe North in October 1964.

Shap

Although not a famous junction or major station, the name Shap conjures up evocative memories for those of us lucky to remember steam on British Railways.

By the early 1960s, this windswept hillside on the Westmorland Fells had become a Mecca for railway photographers keen to capture the raw beauty of steam locomotives powering up the gruelling 1 in 75 gradient from Tebay to Shap Summit – 914 ft above sea level.

Shap is located on the West Coast Main Line between Carnforth and Penrith and the first railway to be built along this route was opened by the Lancaster & Carlisle Railway in 1846. Engineered by Joseph Locke and built by Thomas Brassey, the heavily engineered line between Lancaster and Carlisle took 10,000 navvies only 2½ years to complete.

The hardest approach to Shap Summit is from the south, with the final five miles from Tebay having a gradient of 1 in 75. Here, at Scout Green signal box, just north of Tebay, many famous railway photographers took their finest pictures of Stanier's 'Coronation' Pacifics powering their 12-coach expresses northwards. Although these trains, such as the 'Royal Scot' and the 'Caledonian', normally climbed Shap unassisted, others, such as heavy freights, received help in the rear from banking engines stationed at Tebay. From the north the final approach to Shap Summit was a ten-mile gruelling climb on a gradient of 1 in 125.

With the end of steam on BR less than a year away, the summer and autumn of 1967 saw many railway enthusiasts make their final pilgrimage to witness the spectacle of scheduled steam over Shap.

▲ By 1967 the Tebay 2-6-4 tanks had been replaced by BR Standard Class 4 4-6-0 locos as bankers up Shap. Seen from the cab of banking engine No. 75026 (built at Swindon 1954, withdrawn from Tebay (12E) end 1967), a train of tankers is hauled up Shap Bank by Stanier '8F' 2-8-0 No. 48074 of Heaton Mersey shed (9F) on October 19, 1967.

▼ With its 12-coach train of, all but one, 'blood and custard' coaches BR Standard 'Clan' Class 4-6-2 No 72001 'Clan Cameron' struggles up Shap, banked in the rear by Fowler 2-6-4 tank No. 42424 (built Derby 1934, withdrawn from Stockport Edgeley shed (9B) September 1964), with a Blackpool to Glasgow express in June 1957. Introduced in 1951, the 'Clans' were never a complete success and the ten members of the class were split equally between Carlisle Kingmoor (12A) and Polmadie (66A). 'Clan Cameron' was built at Crewe in 1951 and withdrawn from Polmadie shed at the end of 1962. The last surviving member of the class, No. 72008 'Clan MacLeod' was withdrawn in April 1966. None has been preserved.

▲ Raw Stanier power up Shap – then allocated to Carlisle Upperby (12B), ex-LMS 'Coronation' Class 4-6-2 No. 46225 'Duchess of Gloucester' makes a fine sight as she powers up Shap in the early 1960s. The 'Duchess' was built at Crewe with a streamlined casing in 1938, de-streamlined in 1947 and withdrawn from Upperby in October 1964.

▲ Assisted in the rear by Tebay banker Fairburn 2-6-4 tank No. 42110, 'Black Five' 4-6-0 No. 44677 heads a down freight near Scout Green early on June 1, 1966. A 20mph speed restriction was in place here due to buckling of the track in recent hot weather. The Fairburn tank was built at Derby in 1949 and withdrawn from Tebay shed (12E) only ten days after this photo was taken. The 'Black Five' was built at Horwich in 1950 and withdrawn from Carlisle Kingmoor (12A) in October 1967.

◄ Carlisle Kingmoor 'Black Five' 4-6-0 No. 44727 makes a fine sight as it waits for rear end assistance at Tebay before tackling the climb to Shap Summit in October 1967. Built at Crewe in 1949 No. 44727 was withdrawn from 12A at the end of the month.

Carlisle

Together with Crewe, Carlisle was, and still is, one of the most important railway junctions in Britain. Both are located on the important West Coast Main Line between London Euston and Glasgow.

Carlisle's railway history is incredibly complex with a total of seven different routes and companies reaching the city by 1876. In their order of opening to Carlisle they were: Newcastle & Carlisle Railway (1838); Maryport & Carlisle Railway (1845); Lancaster & Carlisle Railway (1846); Caledonian Railway (Glasgow to Carlisle 1848); North British Railway (Edinburgh to Carlisle 1849); Glasgow, Dumfries & Carlisle Railway (1850 via Gretna Junction on CR); Midland Railway (Settle to Carlisle 1876).

It is amazing that only one of the above routes was closed under the Beeching cuts – the former North British Railway route to Edinburgh via Hawick, known as the Waverley Route, closed in 1969 although that company's branch line to Silloth had already been shut in 1964.

The present imposing façade of Carlisle Citadel was designed by Sir William Tite in 1847 but the station was considerably extended by the Midland Railway on the opening of the Settle & Carlisle route in 1876. By BR days the number of engine sheds had gone from nine to three: Kingmoor (12A), Upperby (12B) and Canal (12C).

Naturally, Carlisle was a paradise for trainspotters especially during the summer months when extra trains were run for the annual Glasgow Fair Holiday and by CTAC (Creative Tourist Agents Conference). With a multitude of routes converging on Carlisle it was possible at least until the mid-1960s to spend a rewarding day at the station – although diesels in the shape of 'Peaks' (Classes 44-46) and English Electric Type 4s (Class 40) had arrived on the scene by 1960 – and spotting a vast range of steam loco classes ranging from the Stanier Pacifics, 'Britannias', 'Clans' and 'Royal Scots' on WCML duties, 'Jubilees' and Black Fives' on trains from Leeds over the Settle & Carlisle to Glasgow St Enoch and ex-LNER 'A3' Pacifics and 'V2' 2-6-2s on trains to Edinburgh via the Waverley Route. Even at night Carlisle was busy with the comings and goings of Travelling Post Office and Anglo-Scottish sleeper trains.

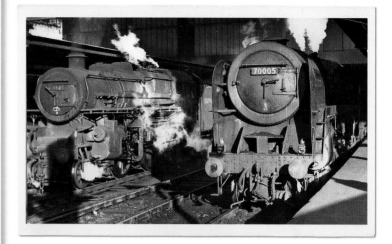

▲ Carlisle Kingmoor locos with two evening departures from Carlisle in 1964 – on the left Ivatt Class 4 2-6-0 No. 43121 waits to depart for the Langholm branch with the last train of the day while, on the right, BR 'Britannia' Class 4-6-2 No. 70005 (minus 'John Milton' nameplate) heads an express for Glasgow. No. 43121 was built at Horwich Works in 1951 and withdrawn from Kingmoor shed in November 1967. Built at Crewe in 1951, No. 70005 initially worked expresses on the GER main line out of Liverpool Street and was withdrawn from Kingmoor in July 1967.

▲ Another Kingmoor loco, this time 'Royal Scot' class 4-6-0 No. 46140 (minus 'The King's Royal Rifle Corps' nameplate), heads the 9am Perth to Euston train at Carlisle on Easter Monday 19 April 1965. Originally built with a parallel Fowler boiler in 1927, this loco was rebuilt in 1952 and withdrawn from Kingmoor in October 1965.

◀ Watched by a couple of trendy '60s onlookers, Stanier 'Black 5' 4-6-0 No. 45055 waits to depart from a wet Carlisle station on 29 July 1966. Blowing off steam in the centre road is Kingmoor's BR 'Britannia' 4-6-2 No. 70038 (minus nameplates).

▶ Steam was very much in evidence on a visit to Carlisle on 1 August 1964. Seen on trains at Carlisle station (left hand column) were 'Jubilee' Nos. 45574, 45581 and 45698, 'Britannia' Nos. 70007, 70017 and 70039 and 'A1' No. 60131 while, afterwards, at Upperby shed were 'Coronation' Nos. 46226, 46237, 46244 and 46250.

◀ Built in 1912, ex-NBR Class 'C-15' 4-4-2 tank No. 67458 was seen on station pilot duties at Carlisle in May 1950. The loco's home shed was Carlisle Canal (12C) from where it was withdrawn in 1956.

Carlisle Kingmoor

12 A

Originally opened by the Caledonian Railway in 1876, Kingmoor went through various rebuilds and improvements under the former owners and, later, by the LMS. Its large allocation of steam locos provided motive power for both freight and passenger services on the WCML and former GSWR/MR routes north and south of Carlisle. Not a difficult shed to visit, Kingmoor was located on the east side of the main line about a 45-minute walk north of Carlisle station.

The shed's large allocation reflected its importance for mixed-traffic locos and included half of the entire class of BR 'Clan' Pacifics and an enormous quantity of 'Black Five' 4-6-0s. Even with the onset of the dieselisation of main line passenger services, by November 1961 Kingmoor's allocation of 127 fairly 'modern' steam locos (made up of 13 different classes) was still at full strength and included in the mixed traffic category were 22 'Crab' 2-6-0s, 48 'Black Five' and nine 'Jubilee' 4-6-0s and five BR 'Clan' Pacifics. By this date Kingmoor was also home to some fairly impressive top link locos, relegated here after being ousted by dieselisation elsewhere, and included a solitary 'Princess', eight 'Coronation' and four 'Britannia' Pacifics. One oddity was a sole member of the ex-WD 2-10-0 Class of heavy freight locos.

The shed managed to stay open nearly to the end of steam on BR, finally closing at the end of 1967.

▲ *A busy scene at Kingmoor shed on July 1, 1962 - in view are a vast array of locomotive types including BR Standard Class 5 4-6-0, 'Jinty' '3F' 0-6-0 tank, Fowler '4F' 0-6-0, 'Crab' 2-6-0, 'Black Five' 4-6-0, 'Coronation' 4-6-2 and 'Britannia' 4-6-2. On the right is 'Jubilee' Class 4-6-0 No. 45691 'Orion' which was withdrawn from Blackpool shed (24E) at the end of 1962.*

▼ *Then allocated to Kingmoor, 'Princess Royal' Class 4-6-2 No. 46201 'Princess Elizabeth' was seen on shed on April 25, 1962 - only six months before withdrawal. Designed by William Stanier this powerful express passenger loco was built at Crewe in 1933. The 'Lizzie' was bought for preservation and initially kept at the Dowty Railway Preservation Society's base at Ashchurch, north of Cheltenham in Gloucestershire. She was subsequently moved to the Bulmer's Railway Centre in Hereford before moving to her final home at the Midland Railway Centre at Butterley in Derbyshire.*

◀ *Steam dreams at Carlisle Kingmoor shed on 29 July 1964 - on my visit I recorded over 80 steam locos including these two 'Jubilees', one 'Royal Scot' and three 'Britannias' Two ex-LNER locos were also present - 'V2' No. 60970 and 'B1' No. 61349 - awaiting their turn on Waverley Route duties.*

92023	
48454	44828	43953
D7584	48297	61349
70039	73007	76085
73106	60970	D3566
44884ᴮ	4581ᴮ	45061
43023	D3172	D3171
44790ᴮ	46166	12080
45455ᴰ	44727ᴮ	44726ᴮ
92017	45105ᴮ	45481ᴮ
70041	70002	47236
73101	92249	44451
43004	44041	45696
45097	47230	45613
44906ᴮ	45491ᴮ	73079
44899ᴮ	44365	45235ᴮ
45295	60835	44902
80113	44677	45364ᴮ
43040	45254	D3114
45164	43040	D5225
44908	47641	D7581
35T 3E	24M	7D

Carlisle Upperby

12B

Located south of Citadel station, there had been a loco shed at Upperby since 1846 when the Lancaster & Carlisle Railway opened for business. Following various enlargements and rebuildings by the L&NWR the depot was completely rebuilt as a large roundhouse and adjacent straight shed by British Railways in 1948 – in fact it was probably the most modern steam shed on BR. With its allocation of mixed-traffic and top link steam locos, Upperby – a 20-minute walk from Citadel station – was a popular shed with trainspotters in the 1950s and early '60s.

Unlike Kingmoor shed, Upperby also became home to a few of the first generation main line diesels which, by November 1961, had reached a total of one named 'Peak' (Class 44) and six English Electric Type 4s (Class 40). By this date Upperby's importance had already started to decline and its steam allocation had dropped to a total of 77, including 23 'Black Five', two 'Royal Scot', three unrebuilt 'Patriot', three rebuilt 'Patriot' and 16 'Jubilee' 4-6-0s and six 'Coronation' Pacifics. The shed closed to steam at the end of 1966.

▲ *Two 'Royal Scot' 4-6-0s, No. 46115 'Scots Guardsman' (since preserved) and No. 46165 'The Ranger (12th London Regt.)', get ready for their next turn of duty at Upperby shed on 13 July 1963.*

▶ *Various withdrawn locos were seen in storage on a visit to Upperby on July 29, 1964 including red-liveried 'Princess Royal' Class 4-6-2 No. 46200 (minus 'The Princess Royal' nameplates). The loco had been withdrawn 20 months earlier, but was finally scrapped in October 1964.*

◀ *During the latter years of steam on the LMR locos were banned from operating under the electrification wires south of Crewe. This restriction was denoted by a yellow diagonal stripe painted on the cabside. Here, complete with stripe and only one month before withdrawal, green-liveried 'Coronation' Class 4-6-2 No. 46237 'City of Bristol' was seen at Upperby shed on August 30, 1964. Behind is '4F' 0-6-0 No. 44009, withdrawn 'Princess Royal' Class 4-6-2 No. 46200 'The Princess Royal', 'Royal Scot' 4-6-0 No. 46110 'Grenadier Guardsman' and rebuilt 'Patriot' 4-6-0 No. 45545 'Planet'.*

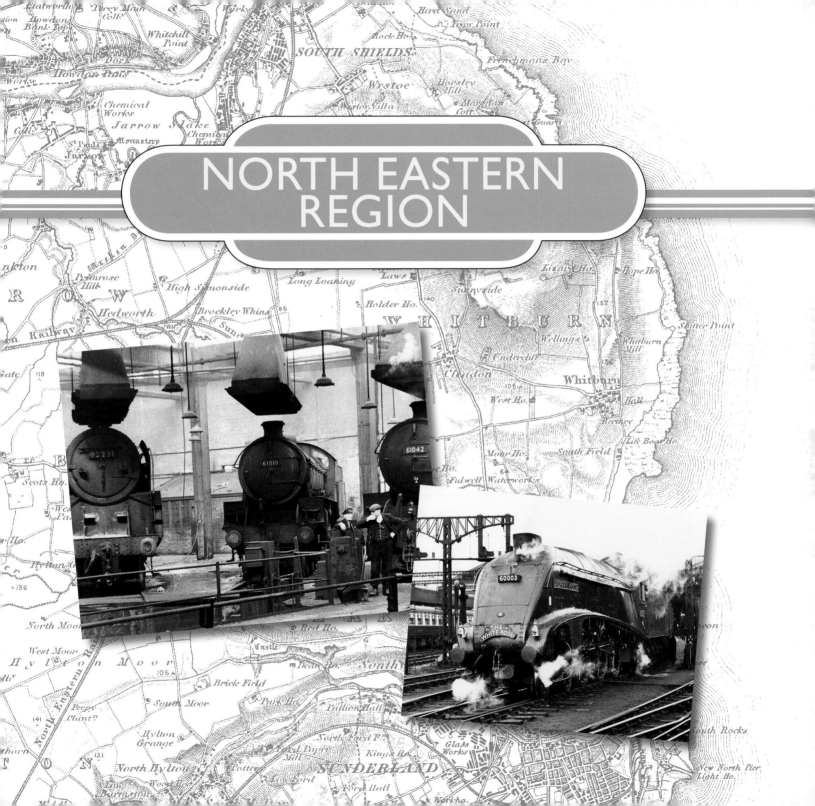

NORTH EASTERN
REGION

Leeds

With two major stations and five engine sheds, Leeds was an important centre for trainspotters up until the mid-1960s.

At that time Leeds boasted two stations, Central and City. Leeds Central opened in 1854 and was operated jointly by the Lancashire & Yorkshire, Great Northern and North Eastern Railways. Until the arrival of the English Electric Type 4s (Class 40), 'Peaks' (Class 45/46) and 'Deltics' (Class 55), trains north to York and Newcastle and south to Doncaster and King's Cross were often in the hands of Copley Hill (56C) shed's allocation of Peppercorn 'A1' Pacifics. Named trains on these routes included 'The Queen of Scots Pullman', 'The Yorkshire Pullman', 'The Harrogate Sunday Pullman', 'The West Riding' and 'The White Rose'. Copley Hill shed closed in 1964 and Central station closed in 1967, with its services diverted to the modernised Leeds City station.

Leeds City station was born out of the combining of New station (a through station opened jointly by the L&NWR and NER in 1869) and the adjacent Wellington station (a terminus opened by the Midland Railway in 1846) by the LMS in 1938. Although City station was modernised in 1967 it was deemed necessary to expand it further to its current 17 platforms when it was rebuilt in 2002. As a branch of the East Coast Main Line, electrification of the route to King's Cross via Doncaster was completed in 1988.

In the late 1950s and early '60s ex-LMS locos such as 'Jubilees', 'Royal Scots' and 'Black Fives' plus a handful of 'Britannias' from Holbeck shed (55A) were a common sight on trains from Leeds City north to Carlisle via the Settle & Carlisle line and south to Sheffield and St Pancras via Chesterfield and to Manchester and beyond. Despite the early introduction of 'Peak' diesels on named trains such as 'The Thames–Clyde Express' and 'The Waverley', steam haulage continued to be seen on trains north from Leeds until the autumn of 1967 when Holbeck shed closed.

▲ Ex-LNER 'D49' Class 4-4-0 No. 62773 'The South Durham' stands at Platform 10 at Leeds City with a stopping train to Harrogate on June 26, 1950. Note the ancient clerestory roof coach immediately behind the engine. Built in 1935, No. 62773 was allocated to 50D (Starbeck) at the time of this photo and was withdrawn in August 1958.

▲ Whitehall Junction, Leeds in the 1950s – 'Royal Scot' Class 4-6-0 No. 46109 'Royal Engineer' heads out of Leeds with the northbound 'Thames–Clyde' express while ex-LNER 'D49' 4-4-0 No. 62764 'The Garth' heads in with a local passenger train from Harrogate. The latter locomotive, also known as a member of the 'Hunt' or 'Shire Class', was built in 1934 and withdrawn in October 1958. 'Royal Engineer' was originally built in 1927, rebuilt with a taper boiler in 1943 and withdrawn in December 1962.

► Magnificently turned-out by King's Cross shed, 'A4' Pacific No. 60003 'Andrew K. McCosh' departs from Leeds Central at 3.32pm with the up 'White Rose' to King's Cross in November 1961. Built in 1937 and originally named 'Osprey' the 'A4' was withdrawn just over a year later at the end of December 1962. 'The Queen of Scots' Pullman train can be seen on the left.

▼ Steam remained active around Leeds up until late 1967 when Holbeck Shed (55A) closed in October. Here, on February 12, 1964, ex-LMS 'Jubilee' Class 4-6-0 No. 45597 'Barbados' marshals parcels vans under the new overall roof at Leeds City station. 'Barbados' had been a Holbeck engine for years and was finally withdrawn in January 1965.

Leeds Holbeck

55A

Opened by the Midland Railway in 1868, Holbeck consisted of two roundhouses and was located on the west side of the Woodlesford line about ½ mile south of Leeds City station.

With a shed code of 20A until 1957, Holbeck was the principal LMR shed in Leeds and provided motive power for trains on the former Midland route north to Carlisle and Glasgow St Enoch via the Settle & Carlisle route and south to Sheffield, St Pancras, Birmingham and even to Bristol.

Although absorbed into the North Eastern Region, Holbeck retained its allocation of ex-LMS locos until the very end when, in October 1967, it became the last shed in Leeds to close to steam.

By November 1961 the shed had lost its 'Royal Scots' but still had an allocation of 59 locos, including only four diesel shunters. Of note were the 15 'Jubilee' 4-6-0s and three 'Britannia' Pacifics.

▲ Holbeck shed on August 23, 1966 - left to right 8F 2-8-0 No. 48283, 'Jubilee' 4-6-0 No. 45697 'Achilles' and 8F 2-8-0 No. 48158. The 'Jubilee', a Holbeck engine by that date, was built at Crewe in 1936 and withdrawn in September 1967.

▼ Under new management - ex-LMS 'Black Five' 4-6-0 No. 44849 stands under Holbeck's coaling plant on October 3, 1948. 'Jubilee' 4-6-0 No. 45561 'Saskatchewan' gets ready to move under on the adjoining track. The pre-Nationalisation 'serif' numberplates on the smokebox doors soon gave way to the more modern 'sans serif' style known to most spotters.

▼ A beautifully clean 'Jubilee' No. 45593 'Kolhapur' is ready for its next turn of duty in 1967. This loco, complete with diagonal yellow stripe on its cab, was withdrawn from Holbeck in October 1967 before being saved for preservation.

Leeds Neville Hall

55 H

Opened by the North Eastern Railway in 1894, Neville Hill shed originally had a code of 50B until 1960 when it changed its code to 55H.

Located on the north side of the Cross Gates line about two miles east of Leeds City station, the shed consisted of a four-road roundhouse shed until 1960 when half of it was rebuilt as a diesel depot. Consequently by 1961 it had a strange mix of ex-LNER steam locos and a large allocation of brand new main line diesels.

Neville Hill's mid-November 1961 allocation totalled 55 locos of which nearly half were diesels – of these 18 were 'Peaks' (Class 45/46). Despite only 29 steam locos being still on the books, eight different classes were represented, notably the four Gresley 'A3' Pacifics.

▶ With a sack tied over its chimney, Gresley 'A3' Pacific No. 60081 'Shotover' awaits its fate in Neville Hill shed in November, 1963. Built at Doncaster in 1924 this loco had been withdrawn from service in October 1962. On the right 'J39' Class 0-6-0 No. 64857 also waits for the summons to the cutter's yard.

▲ With its cabside number barely distinguishable and a grimy nameplate, 'B1' Class 4-6-0 No. 61031 'Reedbuck' was seen at Neville Hill in the summer of 1962. The 'B1' Class had a very short working life - No. 61031 was built in 1947 and withdrawn in November 1964.

◀ Allocated to York shed (50A) Peppercorn 'A1' Class Pacific No. 60154 'Bon Accord' stands over Neville Hill's ash pit in June 1962. Another class with a ridiculously short life - No. 60154 was built in 1949 and withdrawn in October 1965. Although none of this class were preserved we are now fortunate to witness brand new 'A1' Class No. 60163 'Tornado' operating on the main line.

Wakefield

56 A

Located on the east side of the Pontefract line about a 20-minute walk south of Wakefield Kirkgate station, Wakefield shed was a large 10-road dead-end building opened by the Lancashire & Yorkshire Railway in 1893. Formerly coded 25A under the LMR, it was transferred to the North Eastern Region in 1956 when it was rebuilt and became 56A.

Serving a heavily industrialised area of West Yorkshire, the shed provided motive power for heavy freight including the output from many local coal mines. Wakefield's allocation of 64 freight locos in November 1961 reflects its importance in the region. There were eleven different classes represented, among them diesel shunters and two ancient ex-L&YR 3F 0-6-0s dating from 1889. The most numerous classes were the 44 ex-WD 2-8-0s, followed by eight ex-LNER B1 4-6-0s. The shed closed to steam in June 1967.

▲ *A development of the LNWR 'G2' heavy freight loco, 75 of the Fowler 7F 0-8-0 engines were built at Crewe between 1929 and 1932. Here, No. 49610 awaits its next turn of duty at Wakefield on April 30, 1949. The last of this class was withdrawn in 1962.*

▼ *With fireman and driver posing proudly for John Goss's photo, Peppercorn 'A1' Pacific No. 60120 'Kittiwake' looks every bit a powerful machine at Wakefield in June 1962. Then allocated to Copley Hill (56C), this loco was one of the first batch of this class built by BR at Doncaster in 1948. 'Kittiwake' was withdrawn in January 1964 after only 15½ years' service.*

◀ Nearing the end of its days, decrepit 'B1' class 4-6-0 No. 61093 waits its next turn of duty inside Wakefield shed on April 2, 1966.

▼ Built in 1947 'B1' class 4-6-0 No. 61022 'Sassaby' (minus nameplate) is seen here looking rather the worse for wear in its last few months of life at Wakefield on August 23, 1966. This loco was withdrawn in November of that year.

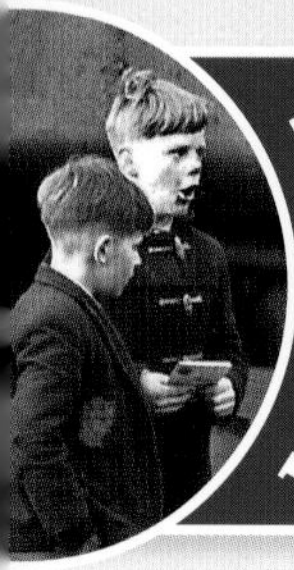

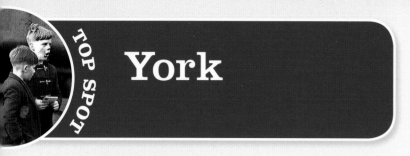

TOP SPOT

York

Astride the East Coast Main Line, York has always been an important rail centre with services south to Doncaster and London King's Cross, north to Newcastle and Edinburgh, west to Leeds and Manchester and Leeds via Harrogate as well as east to Scarborough and to Hull via Market Weighton.

Apart from the last-named route all of the others are still open to traffic. The fiercely independent and ramshackle Derwent Valley Light Railway, with its headquarters at York Layerthorpe, has also long closed apart from a short section at Murton Lane which is now preserved.

The current York station with its curving platforms and overall arched roof was opened by the North Eastern Railway in 1877 and, at that time, was the largest station in the world. The station was enlarged in 1909 and suffered considerable bomb damage during World War II. With its two loco sheds (North and South) and a considerable amount of through traffic, York was a magnet for trainspotters in the late 1950s and early '60s.

Until the arrival of the English Electric Type 4s (Class 40), 'Peaks' (Class 45/46) and 'Deltics' (Class 55), ECML expresses were totally in the hands of ex-LNER Gresley 'A3' and 'A4', Thompson 'A2' and Peppercorn 'A1' Pacifics. Other ex-LNER types that were common at York were the 'B17' (Sandringham Class) and 'B1' 4-6-0s, 'V2' 2-6-2s and, until the late 1950s, the graceful 'D49' (Hunt/Shire Class) 4-4-0s. Trains from the northeast to the Midlands and southwest often changed engines at York with ex-LNER locos giving way to ex-LMS types such as 'Jubilee' or 'Royal Scot' 4-6-0s for their onward journey via Leeds. By the summer of 1963 nearly all ECML passenger services were diesel-hauled, although steam continued in use on freight and local services for a few more years.

Steam was finally ousted in June 1967 when York North shed closed and ECML services remained diesel-hauled, firstly by 'Deltics' and secondly by HSTs, until electrification of the entire route in 1990. Despite this, some services are still operated by old HST sets.

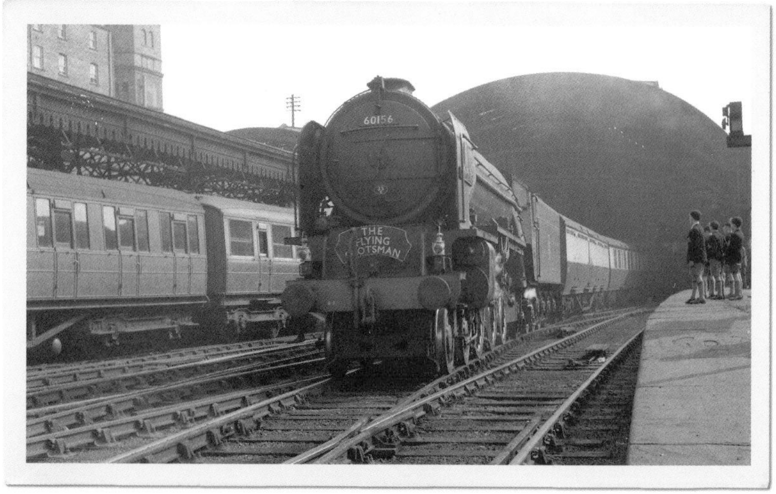

▲ Watched by an excited gaggle of trainspotters and captured magnificently by Gavin Morrison's camera, King's Cross's 'A1' Class 4-6-2 No. 60156 'Great Central' passes non-stop through the centre road at York station with the down 'Flying Scotsman' on 10 April 1954. Built in 1949 and fitted with Timken roller bearings this fine loco was withdrawn in May 1965.

▼ Peppercorn 'A1' Pacific No. 60143 'Sir Walter Scott' leaves York with an up evening express made up of mainly 'blood and custard' stock in March 1957. Built at Darlington in 1949 and fitted with a Kylchap exhaust, this loco had a very short life and was withdrawn in May 1964.

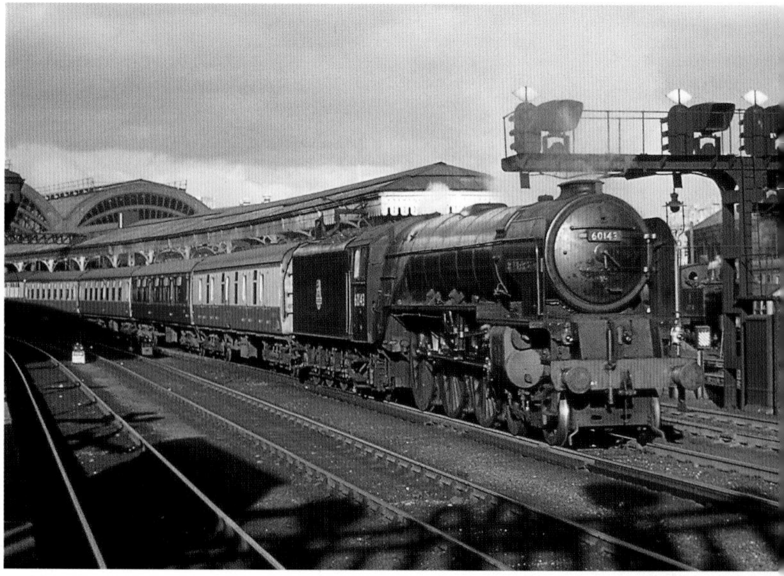

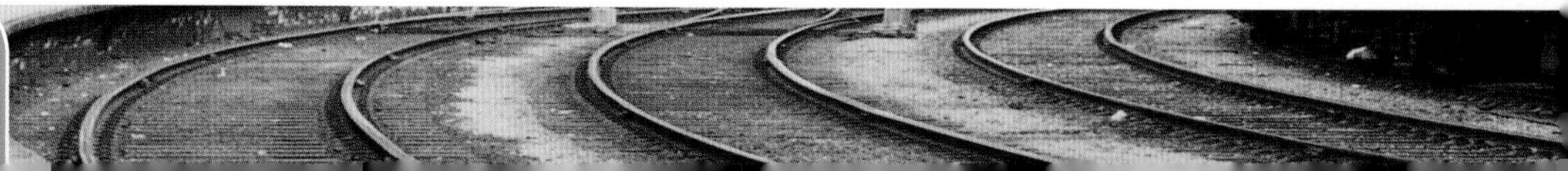

◄ Darlington's rather grimy 'V2' Class 2-6-2 No. 60809 get's the celebrity treatment from a young photographer at York station on 24 June 1961. The loco had one of the longest locomotive names in Britain – 'The Snapper, The East Yorkshire Regiment, The Duke of York's Own'.

▼ Showing off its graceful lines a Gresley 'V2' 2-6-2 accelerates a northbound parcels train away from York c.1960. In the foreground, Class '04/8' 2-8-0 No. 63612 trundles along with a coal train from South Yorkshire. The Class '04/8' were a 1944-rebuild (including a 'B1' boiler and new cab) of the Robinson-designed '01' locos built for the Great Central Railway in 1911. The last members of this class were withdrawn in April 1966.

York

50 A

▼ Gathered around the turntable in York shed one day in May 1964 are (left to right) 'V2' Class 2-6-2 No. 60886; an un-identified WD Austerity; 'B1' Class 4-6-0 No. 61031 'Reedbuck' and Peppercorn 'A1' Class 4-6-2 No. 60146 'Peregrine'. The 'A1', a York loco, was withdrawn in October 1965.

York once boasted two large steam engine sheds: York South, which housed LMS locos and York North, which housed LNER locos. Consisting of two roundhouses, York South was located in the triangle of lines on the west side of the ECML south of York Station. Access was via a boarded crossing from Platform 16.

Due to rationalisation, the shed was closed to steam in 1961 and its allocation moved to North shed. York North consisted of four adjacent sheds – two roundhouses, one dead end shed and one through shed. It was located on the west side of the ECML, a 10-minute walk north of York station

Following the closure of South shed in 1961, North shed's allocation totalled 185 locos including 21 English Electric Type 4 (Class 40) diesels and

36 diesel shunters. The steam roll call included nine ex-LMS locos, two BR Standard 2-6-0s, 11 ex-WD 2-8-0s and 106 ex-LNER locos. Among the latter were nine 'A1' and seven 'A2' Pacifics, 33 'V2' 2-6-2s, 23 'B1' (of which seven were named) and 19 'B16' (nearly all of the remaining members of this class) 4-6-0s and ten 'K1' 2-6-0s.

North Shed closed to steam in the summer of 1967 but operated as a diesel depot until 1984. The buildings and site have now been incorporated as part of the National Railway Museum.

◄ A wintry scene, c.1960 as ex-LNER 'K3' Class 2-6-0 No. 61981 reverses under York's coaling plant. Designed for the Great Northern Railway by Nigel Gresley a total of 193 of these locos were built between 1920 and 1937. Withdrawals took place between 1959 and 1962.

◀ Ex-LMS Stanier 2-cylinder 2-6-4 tank No. 42548, built by the North British Locomotive Company in 1936, poses on the turntable inside York roundhouse on August 25, 1964. On the right, with its smokebox door open for cleaning, is BR Standard 9F 2-10-0 No. 92211 - although designed for hauling freight trains, members of the 9F Class were also known for their smooth running at high speed while hauling passenger trains on the East Coast Main Line.

▶ A handsome lineup at York on an undisclosed date in the 1960s. On the left is Peppercorn 'A1' Pacific No. 60121 'Silurian' while in the foreground 'V2' Class 2-6-2 No. 60876 obscures the identity of the 9F 2-10-0 behind it. Both Nos 60121 and 60876 were allocated to York and both withdrawn in October 1965. Note the visiting SR 'Merchant Navy' on the right!

◀ No doubt the subject of a deep discussion, Doncaster-allocated 'B1' Class 4-6-0 No. 61042 waits to move on to the turntable inside York roundhouse on March 31, 1966. Its shed mates include BR Standard 9F 2-10-0 No. 92231 and fellow 'B1' No. 61019 'Nilghai'. The latter was built in 1947 and withdrawn in March 1967.

LOCATED NEAR NORTH ROAD STATION on the Darlington to Bishop Auckland branch, the Works was about a 30-minute walk from Bank Top station on the ECML.

As well as building many mixed-traffic, freight and shunting locos for the NER, Darlington was also responsible for building the five 'A2' Pacifics designed by Vincent Raven. The first two of these were built by the NER in 1922 with the other three being built after the Big Four Grouping by the LNER in 1924.

With Nigel Gresley as CME, Darlington went on to build a batch of K3 2-6-0s, 52 B17s ('Sandringhams'), D49 4-4-0s ('Hunt/Shire'), 261 'J39' 0-6-0s, six 'K4' 2-6-0s for the West Highland Line, batches of 'V2' 2-6-2s and the 'Hush-Hush' 'W1' 4-6-4 in 1929. Under Edward Thompson the Works built his 'A2/1' Pacifics, a batch of 'B1' 4-6-0s and 30 'L1' 2-6-4 tanks, before continuing with a batch of 22 Peppercorn 'A1' Pacifics, all of which were built under BR management between 1948 and 1949.

After Nationalisation, work continued on building the entire class of 65 BR Standard Class 2 2-6-0s and ten of the BR Standard Class 2 2-6-2 tanks along with a batch of what became known later as the Class 11 diesel shunter. Construction of steam locos at Darlington then ceased but,

▲ By the mid-60s the last few ex-LNER Pacifics to receive works attention were handled at Darlington instead of Doncaster. Here Class 'A2/3' Pacific No. 60522 'Straight Deal' and Class 'A2' Pacific No. 60530 'Sayajirao' are seen inside Darlington North Road Works. No. 60522 was built in 1947 and withdrawn in June 1965. No. 60530 was built at Doncaster in 1948 and spent its short working life allocated to Scottish sheds before being withdrawn from Dundee Tay Bridge (62B) in November 1966.

▶ North Road Works in the 1950s with a motley collection of boilers, ex-NER and ex-LNER locos. Ex-NER J27 0-6-0 No. 65874 is in the left foreground. Introduced in 1906, 36 of the 'J27' Class lasted until the very end of steam on the North Eastern Region operating coal trains. The last 'J27' in service, No. 65894, was withdrawn from Sunderland shed in 1967 and has since been preserved.

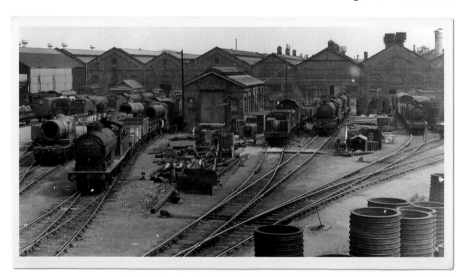

◄ In ex-works condition ex-NER 'Q7' 0-8-0 No. 63460 trundles past Darlington Works 1930s-style office on September 20, 1963 having been saved from the scrapyard the year before and preserved as part of the National Collection. Introduced in 1919 only 15 of these heavy freight locos were built and ended their lives allocated to Tyne Dock (52H) for hauling heavy iron-ore trains to Consett. They were all withdrawn in 1962 and replaced by BR Standard 9F 2-10-0s.

from 1953, the Works continued to build diesels with batches of the Class 08, Class 09 and Class 10 diesel shunters. Main line diesel loco production at Darlington consisted of a batch of BR Sulzer Type 2 (Class 24/25). The three unusual pairs of Class 13 'cow and calf' shunters were also built at Darlington in 1965 for use at the Tinsley Marshalling Yard in Sheffield.

Darlington Works closed in 1966 – however, that is not the final story as the brand new 'A1' Pacific No. 60163 'Tornado' was out-shopped from the new locomotive works in Hopetown Lane. Costing £3 million, paid for by donations and sponsors, 'Tornado' made its first moves under steam in July 2008.

▲ Introduced in 1949, a total of 70 Peppercorn 'K1' Class 2-6-0s were built for the Eastern and North Eastern regions of BR by the North British Locomotive Company. Here, No. 62041 in gleaming lined BR black poses for our photographer outside Darlington Works after a major overhaul in 1964. In 1967 No. 62005 became the last engine of this class to be withdrawn. It has since been preserved.

◄ 'Flying Scotsman' was the most famous Gresley 'A3' Pacific, but a contender for second place was No. 60100 'Spearmint'. For years she was the pride of Edinburgh Haymarket (64B) and features prominently in railway folklore. Dieselisation of the East Coast Main Line caused 'Spearmint' to be transferred to Edinburgh St Margaret's (64A) in 1962 where she remained until withdrawn in June 1965. She was despatched promptly to Darlington and breaking up proceeded in July. This sad picture shows the thoroughbred partly dismantled but with nameplates still in position.

Darlington

In addition to the ex-North Eastern Railway Works and locomotive shed, Darlington possessed (and still does) two railway stations.

▲ Far from home. Ex-SR 'Schools' Class 4-4-0 No. 30925 'Cheltenham' and ex-LMS '2P' 4-4-0 No. 40646 pause at Bank Top station on May 13, 1962 at the head of an RCTS special train, 'The East Midlander', before returning to Nottingham. 'Cheltenham' has since been preserved and is part of the National Collection at the NRM, York.

North Road, on the line to Wearhead via Bishop Auckland and to Penrith via Barnard Castle, is the more historic of the two stations as it is the site of the terminus of the world's first public railway – the Stockton & Darlington Railway that opened in 1825. It is also located close to the site of the former North Eastern Railway Works. However, the only trains that stop here now are those on the Bishop Auckland branch.

Bank Top station, however, is located on the East Coast Main Line, and the present building dates from 1887, when it replaced a much smaller station. Still busy with services on the electrified ECML and to Middlesbrough, Redcar and Bishop Auckland, Bank Top was once a great place to spot not only the Gresley Pacifics on main line expresses such as 'The Talisman', 'The Northumbrian', 'The Heart of Midlothian' and 'The Aberdonian' and L1 2-6-2 tanks on stopping trains to Richmond, but also BR Standard Class 4 and Ivatt Class 2 2-6-0s on the trans-Pennine route to Penrith. Freight traffic from industrial Teeside and the Durham coalfields was particularly heavy and brought many different types of ex-NER and LNER freight locos to the Darlington area. The end of steam came in Spring 1966 when the nearby Darlington shed (51A) closed.

▲ By 1964 the East Coast Main Line expresses had been totally dieselised. On February 12 English Electric Type 5 'Deltic' (Class 55) D9013 'The Black Watch' pauses at Bank Top station with the southbound 'Tees-Tyne Pullman'. One of a class of 22 locos built by English Electric between 1961 and 1962, D9013 was finally withdrawn from service in December 1981.

◄ When the grey accountants declared steam-hauled trains uneconomic, no consideration was given to the fact that they were a source of healthy occupation for millions of youngsters, a fact confirmed by this picture of Darlington Bank Top station looking north from the south end of the Up main platform on October 10, 1953. Gresley 'A4' Pacific No. 60006, 'Sir Ralph Wedgwood' heads 'The Northumbrian' alongside one of the lovely Class 'A8' 4-6-2 tanks which were Gresley re-builds of Raven 'D' Class 4-4-4 tanks.

Darlington

51 A

With its important railway works, large engine shed and Bank Top station sitting astride the East Coast Main Line, Darlington was a favourite destination for trainspotters. There had been an engine shed in Darlington since 1825 when the world's first public railway, the Stockton & Darlington, was opened. This shed was located at North Road close to where the North Eastern Railway later built its Works.

▲ *Heaton shed's 'V2' 2-6-2 No. 60868 makes a fine sight at Darlington shed on 29 September 1962 after a major overhaul in Darlington Works.*

◄ *Looking in almost immaculate condition Darlington-allocated 'V2' 2-6-2 No. 60885 simmers outside the shed on September 20, 1963. This loco was still on the shed's books in April 1965 and was one of the last batch to be withdrawn. To the left is ex-works ex-NER 'Q7' 0-8-0 No. 63460 which had been saved from the scrapyard the year before and preserved as part of the National Collection.*

The main shed at Darlington, consisting of a roundhouse opened in 1866 by the NER and a nine-road through shed opened in 1940 by the LNER, was located on the east side of the main line only a five minute walk north from Bank Top station. Its allocation of mainly mixed-traffic and freight locos reflected the importance of freight traffic, particularly from Teeside, in this industrialised region of northeast England. In addition the shed also supplied locos for secondary route passenger services to Penrith via Barnard Castle and Stainmore Summit, the Richmond branch and to Teeside via Stockton.

In the Autumn of 1961, prior to the closure of the trans-Pennine route, Darlington's allocation totalled 68 steam locos plus 27 diesel shunters. Twelve different classes of steam locos were represented of which the two 'A3' Pacifics – 60053 'Sansovino' and 60075 'St Frusquin' – were the stars of the shed. There were also nine 'B1' 4-6-0s (including two named – 61032 'Marmion' and 61037 'Redgauntlet'), a solitary named 'V2' 2-6-2 (60809 'The Snapper, The East Yorkshire Regiment, The Duke of York's Own'), 11 'K1' 2-6-0s, 15 J94 saddle tanks and 12 ex-WD 2-8-0s. Darlington shed finally closed its doors to steam in Spring 1966.

◄ *Fitted with German-style smoke deflectors and a double Kylchap exhaust, Gresley 'A3' Class 4-6-2 No. 60045 'Lemberg' reverses up to the turntable on August 11, 1964. This handsome loco was originally built by the LNER as an 'A1' Pacific in 1924 and rebuilt as an 'A3' in 1927. Withdrawal took place in November 1964.*

▼ *Allocated to Leeds Neville Hill (55H), 'K1' Class 2-6-0 No. 62007 was seen in ex-works condition at Darlington in April 1965. Built by the North British Locomotive Co. a total of 70 engines of this class entered service between May 1949 and March 1950. They had all been withdrawn by 1967 but one, No.62005, was saved for preservation.*

Newcastle

Designed by John Dobson with three curved and arched train shed roofs, Newcastle Central was opened in 1850 as a joint station for the York, Newcastle & Berwick Railway and the Newcastle & Carlisle Railway.

Along with other constituent companies, these soon merged to become the North Eastern Railway. The station was approached over the High Level Bridge designed by Robert Stephenson to carry both road and rail over the River Tyne. However, until the King Edward VII Bridge was built in 1906, through trains on the East Coast Main Line had to reverse at Central Station. The station also underwent an extension in the 1890s and a suburban third-rail electric train service to Tynemouth started operating from the east side in 1904. The NER claimed that the complex rail junction with its multitude of diamond crossings on the approach to the station was the largest in the world.

Despite the introduction of diesels on ECML trains, Central station was still popular with trainspotters in the late 1950s and early '60s. For a few years the new English Electric Type 4 (Class 40), 'Peak' (Class 45/46) and 'Deltic' (Class 55) diesels could be seen rubbing shoulders with Gresley's magnificent 'A3' and 'A4' Pacifics, along with Thompson 'A2' and Peppercorn 'A1' Pacifics. Named trains were a'plenty and included 'The Flying Scotsman', which made its one scheduled intermediate stop at Central, the morning and afternoon 'Talisman', 'The Northumbrian', 'The Heart of Midlothian', 'The Queen of Scots Pullman' and 'The Tees-Tyne Pullman'.

Alongside these stars of the show were the mixed traffic 'B1' 4-6-0s, 'V2' 2-6-2s and more humble locos including 'V1' and 'V3' 2-6-2 tanks on local and empty coaching stock duties, and for some years Gateshead's diminutive 'J72' 0-6-0 tanks (vintage 1898), some repainted in LNER green, could be seen pottering around Central station on pilot duties. Now all this is gone – the 'Deltics' were replaced by HSTs in the late 1970s and they, in turn, were replaced by Intercity 225 trains on completion of ECML electrification in 1991.

The suburban electric trains to Tynemouth were withdrawn in 1967 and replaced by diesel multiple units but these were also withdrawn in 1980 when the Tyne & Wear Metro commenced service. Consequently the east side of the station has now become a car park.

▲ Young spotters watch the arrival of 'The Queen of Scots Pullman' in Newcastle headed by ex-LNER 'A2/1' Class Pacific No. 60510 'Robert the Bruce'. One of four locos built at Darlington in January 1945 as a Pacific version of Gresley's 'V2' 2-6-2 this loco spent much of its life at Haymarket shed (64B) and was withdrawn in November 1960.

◀ Gresley 'A3' Class Pacific No. 60051 'Blink Bonny' restarts vigorously from Newcastle on August 8, 1964. Allocated to Heaton shed (52B), this loco was built in 1924 and withdrawn only three months after this photo was taken, in November 1964.

◀ Ex-LNER 'A3' Class Pacific No. 60099 'Call Boy' enters Newcastle Central with an up Car-Carrier train in September 1961. An English Electric Type 4 (Class 40) waits to take over the train to London (Holloway). The cost of conveying a car and its driver (2nd Class) from Newcastle to London was then £9 10s (single). A Haymarket (64B) loco at this time, 'Call Boy' was built in 1930 and withdrawn in October 1963.

▶ Peppercorn 'A1' Pacific No. 60155 'Borderer' waits to depart from Newcastle on August 8, 1964. One of five 'A1s' fitted with Timken roller bearings this loco was built at Doncaster in 1949 and withdrawn in October 1965. Needing a works overhaul on average every 120,000 miles these five locos were probably amongst the most reliable steam engines ever built in Britain.

Gateshead

The principal depot for East Coast Main Line motive power in the Newcastle area, there had been an engine shed at Gateshead since 1839. Located on the north side of the line west of Gateshead West station, the depot finally ended up with four square adjoining roundhouses and a straight three-road shed for the larger North Eastern Railway Pacifics. By the late 1950s and early '60s Gateshead, with its impressive allocation of Gresley Pacifics, held a magnetic attraction for trainspotters. However, by late 1961 the writing was on the wall for these magnificent locos as increasing numbers of main line diesels arrived at the shed. By this time there were 78 diesels allocated including four

▲ Ex-LNER Class 'J39' 0-6-0 No. 64701 takes a drink of water at Gateshead on June 5, 1950. Built in 1926 this standard LNER goods loco was allocated to 52A at that time and was withdrawn from Sunderland South Dock (52G) in October 1962.

'Peaks' (Class 45), 26 English Electric Type 4 (Class 40) and six of the mighty 'Deltic' (Class 55).

This invasion had seriously reduced the steam allocation which, by now, was down to a shadow of its former self with only 42 locos. Despite this, there were still some beauties, including eight 'A4' and 11 'A3' Gresley Pacifics and some old-timers in the shape of six of Worsdell's NER J72 0-6-0 tanks of 1898 vintage, some of which had been repainted in their old NER livery for their duties as station pilot at Newcastle Central station. Three of Worsdell's 1902 NER 'N10' 0-6-2 tanks were still on the books, but they faced imminent withdrawal.

Part of the depot was converted to a diesel maintenance depot in 1964 and the shed finally closed to steam in the Autumn of 1965. The diesel depot was subsequently closed in 1991 following electrification of the ECML to Edinburgh.

▲ Seen here in Gateshead shed in June 1950, ex-LNER Class 'Y1' 0-4-0 geared steam loco No. 68141 was built by the Sentinel wagon works in 1929. Despite withdrawals in the 1950s several survived as departmental locos until the 1960s. One member of this class, No. 68153 has been preserved.

▶ Designed by W Worsdell for the North Eastern Railway Class 'G5' 0-4-4 tank No. 67260 was a visitor to 52A when pictured here in June 1950. Built in 1896 this loco spent its last years operating out of Sunderland South Dock shed and was withdrawn from there in 1952.

▲ A powerful line-up inside Gateshead diesel depot on August 28, 1972. From left to right are Class 40 No. 346 (built in 1961, withdrawn in December 1980), 'Deltic' Class 55 No. 9017 'The Durham Light Infantry' (built 1961, withdrawn December 1981) and Class 47 No. 1518 (built in 1963, later renumbered 47419 and withdrawn in 1987). The name of the 'Deltic' was originally carried by 'V2' Class 2-6-2 No. 60964.

▼ With its smokebox door hinges picked out in silver, ex-LNER 'Class 'V3' 2-6-2 tank No. 67628, previously allocated to Helensburgh shed (65H), was photographed at Gateshead on November 24, 1962. The last surviving 'V3s' were withdrawn in 1964.

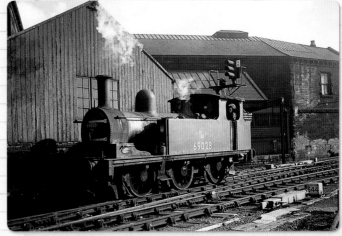

▲ Originally introduced by the NER as far back as 1898 a final batch of 'J72' 0-6-0 tanks were built at Darlington between 1949 and 1951. Here No. 69028, the last member of this class to be built and painted in NER green for its station pilot duties at Newcastle Central, was photographed at Gateshead on July 24, 1964 shortly before withdrawal.

SCOTTISH REGION

Glasgow Central

Opened by the Caledonian Railway in August 1879, Glasgow Central became the major city terminus for local trains to Clydeside and the company's southerly route to Edinburgh as well as the important Anglo-Scottish expresses via Carlisle.

Although not as architecturally appealing as the nearby Glasgow & South Western Railway's St Enoch station, Central station during the 1950s and early '60s daily witnessed the humble comings-and-goings of the ex-LMS Fairburn and BR Standard tanks on intensive local services. Central had a much more glitzy side to it than just this in the form of the Anglo-Scottish expresses such as the 'Royal Scot', 'Mid-Day Scot' and 'The Caledonian' as well as overnight sleeper and TPO trains to the south. Stars of this show were primarily the Stanier 'Coronation' Class Pacifics which were ousted in the early '60s by English Electric Type 4 diesels (BR Class 40) and later by the English Electric Type 4 'Hoovers' or what later became BR Class 50. Needless to say these, in turn, were all swept away on electrification of the West Coast Main Line in 1974. Tilting electric multiple units are now the order of the day!

▲ A quiet moment at Glasgow Central in the 1950s as a solitary passenger on Platform 7 patiently awaits her train and shafts of sunlight penetrate the gloomy interior.

▶ 'Blood and Custard' days at Glasgow Central in April 1955 as Polmadie's 'Royal Scot' Class 4-6-0 No. 46105 'Cameron Highlander' departs with a train for Edinburgh Princes Street.

▲ Watched by a lone trainspotter, 'Polmadie's immaculate 'Coronation' Class 4-6-2 No. No. 46223 'Princess Alice' prepares to leave Glasgow Central with the up 'The Royal Scot' in the late 1950s.

ON SHED
Glasgow Polmadie

66 A

▶ Allocated to 66A, ex-LMS 'Coronation' 4-6-2 No. 46224 'Princess Alexandra' is seen at rest at its home shed in April 1962. Built at Crewe with a streamlined casing in 1937, this loco was de-streamlined and fitted with smoke deflectors in 1946. After 26 years service hauling heavy expresses on the West Coast Main Line it was withdrawn from Polmadie in October 1963.

The principal shed for the West Coast Main Line out of Glasgow Central station, Polmadie was originally opened by the Caledonian Railway in 1875. Located on the east side of the WCML about a 40 minute walk south of Central station, the shed went through several rebuilds under LMS and BR ownership.

During the 1950s the shed's allocation of top link locos such as ex-LMS 'Princess' and 'Coronation' Class Pacifics provided motive power for some famous Anglo-Scottish expresses such as 'The Royal Scot', 'The Mid-day Scot' and 'The Caledonian'. Despite the onslaught of dieselisation in other parts of Scotland by the early 1960s, even as late as October 1961 Polmadie had no allocation of the new main line diesels.

Apart from 22 diesel shunters, it was still an all-steam shed with a total allocation of 136 locos representing 18 different classes. Of note were representatives of no less than five former Caledonian Railway classes, five 'Royal Scot' 4-6-0s, nine 'Coronation', three 'Britannia'

◀ A visit to Polmadie shed on 29 March 1964 revealed the sudden invasion of Scotland by those dreadful Clayton diesels. Also on shed were a few more worthy but nearly life-expired steam locos including 'A2' Nos. 60522 and 60530, rebuilt 'Patriot' No. 45531, 'Royal Scot' No. 46155 and the final Ivatt 'Coronation', No. 46257.

and five 'Clan' Pacifics. A visit to the shed at the end of March 1964 revealed a large allocation of the extremely short-lived Clayton Type 1 (Class 17) diesels alongside 41 steam locos – stars of the show then were the three ex-LNER 'A2' Pacifics – 60522, 60530 and 60535 – reallocated to Polmadie following dieselisation of the East Coast Main Line. Sadly, by this date there was just one solitary 'Coronation' Pacific (46257 'City of Salford') and one 'Royal Scot' (46155 'The Lancer') on shed.

Polmadie finally closed to steam in May 1967 and a part of it went on to be utilised as a diesel depot.

Glasgow Buchanan Street

One of four railway termini in Glasgow, Buchanan Street station was opened in 1849 as the terminus of the Caledonian Railway.

▲ The end is nigh – 'A4' Pacific No. 60024 'Kingfisher' reverses slowly out of Buchanan Street after hauling a three-hour express from Aberdeen on August 23, 1966. Allocated to Ferryhill (61B) the 'A4' was one of the last two members of this class (the other being No. 60019 'Bittern') to remain in service until withdrawal two weeks later.

P rior to closure the station provided services to Edinburgh, Aberdeen via Perth and Forfar, Inverness via Perth, Oban via Stirling and Callander and Dundee via Perth. Although diesels in the shape of Birmingham R. C. & W. Type 2 (Class 26/27) and the unlamented North British Type 2 (Class 21) had started appearing on some services in the early 1960s, Buchanan Street still drew trainspotters from far and wide up to the mid-'60s. The reason for this was the transfer of a number of Gresley 'A4' Pacifics to Aberdeen Ferryhill shed (61B) in 1962 following their displacement by diesels – notably 'Deltics' – on the ECML. Performing their swan song, these magnificent beasts were soon hauling the Buchanan Street to Aberdeen (via Forfar) three-hour expresses, a job they continued to perform very well, along with the occasional 'A2' Pacific, until the Autumn of 1966.

The Scottish Region timetable for Summer 1964 lists four named trains on this 153-mile route: 'The Grampian', 'The Bon Accord', 'The Granite City' and 'The St Mungo'. Until 1963 the Oban via Callander trains were usually hauled by 'Black Five' 4-6-0s but these were replaced by double-headed North British Type 2s until a landslip brought about the early closure of the Dunblane to Crianlarich section on September 27, 1965. After this date Oban trains were diverted to run from Queen Street over the West Highland Line via Crianlarich. However, 'Black Fives' and BR Standard Class 5 4-6-0s could still be seen at work on trains from Buchanan Street to Perth, Stirling and Dundee up until the end. The station closed on November 7, 1966 and has since been demolished.

▶ Seen here at Buchanan Street on July 26, Peppercorn Class 'A2' Pacific No. 60532 'Blue Peter' was also a regular on the three-hour expresses from Aberdeen in 1966. Allocated to Dundee Tay Bridge shed (62B) until withdrawal at the end of that year, 'Blue Peter' was saved from the cutter's torch by an appeal launched in conjunction with the BBC TV children's programme of the same name.

Glasgow Queen Street

Opened in 1842 by the Edinburgh & Glasgow Railway, Queen Street High Level station became the Glasgow terminus of the North British Railway (later the LNER).

G lasgow Queen Street provided services to Edinburgh Waverley, Fife and, from August 1894, on the newly-opened West Highland line to Fort William and Mallaig. Suburban services to the east and west called at Queen Street Low Level station. With its rather cramped layout and overall glazed arched roof, High Level station was approached through a tunnel down a 1 in 42 incline. Until 1909 departing trains were hauled by a powerful winch up the incline as far as Cowlairs. After this date trains were banked in the rear by tank locos until the end of steam in 1963 when modern diesels were able to haul their trains up the incline unassisted.

Along with Peppercorn Class A1 Pacifics at the head of two named trains – 'The North Briton' to Leeds City and 'The Queen of Scots Pullman' to King's Cross (both via Edinburgh Waverley), the West Highland Line departures were the highlight of a day's trainspotting at Queen Street. Motive power (often double-headed), supplied by Eastfield depot (65A) for these trains ranged from the ex-NBR 'D34' 4-4-0s (known as 'Glens') and ex-Great Northern Railway 'K2' 2-6-0s (known as 'Lochs') to the ex-LNER 'K4' 2-6-0s and the more modern 'K1' 2-6-0s, ex-LMS 'Black Fives' and BR Standard Class 5 4-6-0s. However, by 1960, with the introduction of the Birmingham R. C. & W. Type 2 (Class 27) and North British Type 2 (Class 21) diesels already underway, the writing was on the wall for steam services out of Queen Street. It became the first terminus in Glasgow to see the end of steam workings and, in November 1966, also took over the services that formerly terminated at the neighbouring Buchanan Street station.

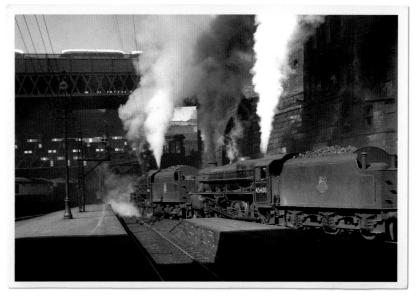

▲ The cramped confines of Gasgow's Queen Street station echo to the sound of the double-headed 3.36pm train to Mallaig leaving behind Stanier 'Black 5' 4-6-0s Nos. 44908 and 45400 on 18 September 1954 – immediately ahead lies a tunnel and the fearsome 1-in-41 Cowlairs Bank.

▲ Ex-LMS Stanier Class 5 4-6-0 No. 44973 waits to depart from Queen Street with a train for Fort William in April 1957. This photo clearly shows the operational problems caused by long trains waiting in the station's short platforms. Built at Crewe in 1946, the 'Black Five' spent some time allocated to Fort William shed (63B), but after dieselisation of the West Highland line ended up at Carstairs (66E), from where it was withdrawn in September 1965.

ON SHED Glasgow Eastfield 65A

▶ Around 9.10am and it's clocking on time at Eastfield shed in September 1954. Plenty of locomotive activity too, as an assortment of ex-NBR, GCR, GNR and LNER locomotives including Classes 'D11', 'D94' 'K2' and 'K4' get ready for a hard day's work.

▲ Minus its shed code plate, Thompson Class 'A2/3' 4-6-2 No. 60512 'Steady Aim' languishes inside Eastfield shed on March 29, 1964. Built at Doncaster in 1946 this loco was withdrawn from Polmadie (66A) in June 1965.

▶ The Glasgow and Edinburgh shed bash of March 29, 1964 was an exhausting but exhilarating trip. At Eastfield (left hand column) there were still three Class 'J37' 0-6-0s on shed along with 'A2/3' 4-6-2 No. 60512. At nearby St Rollox there were three BR Standard Caprotti 4-6-0s, 'A4' 4-6-2 No. 60011 and 'A2' 4-6-2 No. 60527.

The principal engine shed for the North British Railway in Glasgow, Eastfield was a large 14-road through shed which opened in 1904 and was located on the east side of the line about a 20-minute walk north of Cowlairs station.

With dieselisation of the West Highland Line already well underway, by October 1961 Eastfield had already lost many of its steam star performers for that scenic route such as the 'D34' 4-4-0s ('Glens'), 'K2' 2-6-0s ('Lochs') and 'K4' 2-6-0s. By that date they had been replaced by 11 Birmingham R. C. & W. Type 2s (Class 27) and 38 of the unsuccessful and short-lived North British Type 2s (Class 21) in addition to 25 English Electric Type 1 (Class 20) and 25 diesel shunters.

The shed's steam allocation then totalled 58, made up of nine different classes including examples of five ex-NBR types – 'D94' 4-4-0 (the last remaining 'Glen'), 'J37' 0-6-0, 'J36' 0-6-0 (1888 vintage), 'J83' 0-6-0 and 'N15' 0-6-2 tanks (used as Cowlairs bankers out of Queen Street station). Other classes included ten 'Black Five', seven 'B1' 4-6-0s and four BR Standard Class 5 4-6-0s. A visit to the shed in March 1964 revealed a total of 111 locomotives of which only 40 were steam.

Eastfield shed finally closed to steam in November 1966 and was replaced by a diesel depot which itself was closed in 1992. The only sub-shed was at Arrochar on the West Highland Line. It closed in October 1959.

▼ Although Eastfield closed to steam in 1966, it continued as a diesel depot until 1992. Here one of the named Scottish Class '37's No. 37043 'Loch Lomond' stands inside the depot on March 6, 1982.

▲ An interesting line-up at Eastfield on May 19, 1964. From left to right: 'A4' Class 4-6-2 No. 60010 'Dominion of Canada' (built in 1937, withdrawn from Ferryhill (61B) in May 1965 and since preserved as a static exhibit in Canada); ex-LMS Hughes 'Crab' 2-6-0 No. 42803 visiting from Ayr (67C) (built at Crewe in 1928 and withdrawn in December 1966); ex-LMS rebuilt 'Patriot' Class 4-6-0 No. 45512 'Bunsen' minus centre driving wheel and linkages (built at Crewe in 1932, rebuilt in 1948 and withdrawn in March 1965).

◄ Having just emerged after overhaul from nearby Cowlairs Works in late March 1964, 'Black Five' 4-6-0 No. 45312 looks very handsome in lined BR black livery. One of a batch built by Armstrong Whitworth in 1937 this loco survived until the very last months of steam on BR being withdrawn from Bolton shed (26C) in June 1968. Eighteen members of this class have since been preserved.

Glasgow St Enoch

With its arched wrought iron and glazed roof, Glasgow St Enoch was by far the most impressive terminus station in the city.

Opened in May 1876, it later became the headquarters of the Glasgow & South Western Railway and the starting point for services to Renfrewshire, Ayrshire and Dumfriesshire and Stranraer (for Northern Ireland), as well as Anglo-Scottish services via Dumfries, Carlisle and the Midland Railway route to Leeds and London St Pancras via the Settle & Carlisle route.

The principal named train was the 'Thames-Clyde Express' which, in the summer of 1964, took 8 hours 50 minutes on its journey from St Pancras. Haulage of this train was normally undertaken by one of Stanier's ex-LMS 'Jubilee' Class 4-6-0s until the early '60s when 'Peak' (Class 45/45) diesels took over. Sadly, St Enoch was closed on June 27, 1966 and has since been demolished – what a waste! Surviving services were transferred to Central station.

▲ Although closed a month before to passenger services, St Enoch continued to be used for a while by mail and parcels trains. Here, BR Standard Class 4 2-6-0 No. 76093, allocated to Corkerhill (67A), carries out station pilot duties at Platform 10 of St Enoch on July 27, 1966.

▶ A busy scene at St Enoch in the mid-1950s with 'Black Five' 4-6-0 No. 44856 waiting to depart with its train of 'blood and custard' coaches for Dumfries and Carlisle. Built at Crewe in 1944 this loco was withdrawn in February 1967.

ST. ENOCH - CARLISLE 1/8/64

D228 central	D2761	92012
76114	44993	48157
80025	76073	72009
80005	45432	73809
80109	45456	45065
45012	45463	45118
45675	76672	44828
D19	46479	45600
45480	D3926	45573
76091	45467	70037
45120	D76	D5192
77017	D87	73060
D3413	73122	D5110
46235	45655	45460
77015	43027	CARLISLE 70002
44900	73103	44901
46450	60522	44995
45629!	45185	44683
44995	44624	D310
45225	46792	43023
5ST	8M	2D

◀ With less than two years to go before closure, St Enoch station was still virtually all steam (apart from dmus) on August 1, 1964 – seen in or near the station were 'Jubilee' Nos. 45675 and 45629 and 'Coronation' No. 46235. On the ensuing journey down to Carlisle via Kilmarnock and Dumfries we were hauled by D87 but, apart from one other diesel, all trains that we saw were steam-hauled – these included 'Jubilee' Nos. 45573, 45600 and 45655, 'A2/3' No. 60522, 'Clan' No. 72009 and 'Britannia' No. 70037. From Carlisle we travelled back to Glasgow Central on the delayed 'Royal Scot' headed by 'Britannia' No. 70002, arriving an hour late.

▲ St Enoch's fabulous arched glass roof can be seen in its full glory here in this photo taken just prior to closure in 1966. A couple of DMUs wait in the central platforms with services to Ayrshire while a BR Sulzer Type 4 (later Class 45) waits at the head of an express for the south via Dumfries and Carlisle. This scene has now completely disappeared.

Glasgow Corkerhill

67 A

Built in what was then a rural location by the Glasgow & South Western Railway, Corkerhill shed opened in 1896. It was located on the south side of the line between St Enoch and Paisley Canal and was only a five-minute walk east from Corkerhill station. At the same time the G&SWR also built an adjacent village to house the 112 employees of the shed and their families.

Rebuilt by BR in 1954, the six-road through shed provided motive power for main line services on former G&SWR routes from Glasgow St Enoch. These included services to Renfrewshire, Ayrshire and Dumfriesshire and Stranraer (for Northern Ireland) as well as Anglo-Scottish expresses (such as 'The Thames-Clyde Express') via Dumfries, Carlisle and the Midland Railway route to Leeds and London St Pancras via the Settle & Carlisle route.

▲ *A grandstand view of Corkerhill taken on September 1, 1954. Ex-LMS locos predominate, notably the three 4P Compound 4-4-0s in the front row. Of these two, Nos 41133 and 41142, are identifiable with an ex-Caledonian Railway Class '29' 0-6-0 tank sandwiched between them. No. 41133 was built at Horwich Works in 1926 and was withdrawn from Corkerhill at the end of September 1954. No 41142 was built by the North British Locomotive Company in 1925 and withdrawn from Corkerhill in July 1956.*

Corkerhill's October 1961 allocation totalled 81 locos of which 71 were steam and contained a large percentage of BR Standard types. Of note was a solitary ex-LMS 2P 4-4-0, 14 'Black Five', ten 'Jubilee' and ten BR Standard Class 5 4-6-0s, eight BR Standard Class 4 2-6-0s and 19 BR Standard Class 4 2-6-4 tanks.

A visit to the shed in late March 1964 revealed 44 steam locomotives plus six diesel shunters and (a sign of the times!) two 'Peak' diesels (Class 45) – D14 and D18. Included in the steam tally were three 'Royal Scots' and a 'Jubilee'. Later that year, in early August 1964, another visit revealed a total of only 23 locomotives – all steam except for one diesel shunter – which included visiting 'A2' Pacific No. 60535 'Hornets Beauty'.

St Enoch closed in June 1966 and all former G&SWR services were transferred to Central station. Corkerhill closed to steam in May 1967 but continued in use as a diesel depot.

▲ *Kingmoor's 'Jubilee 4-6-0 No. 45588 'Kashmir' waits its next turn of duty down the G&SWR main line at Corkerhill shed on 10 August 1961.*

◀ Several 'Royal Scot' 4-6-0s, minus name and numberplates, were spotted stored out of use at Corkerhill during a visit on March 29, 1964. Here, No. 46104 'Scottish Borderer', built in 1927 and rebuilt in 1946, looks decidedly the worse for wear 15 months after withdrawal.

◀ Keeping No. 46104 company on 'death row' at Corkerhill was fellow class member No. 46102 'Black Watch', which had also been withdrawn 15 months earlier. The name (with the prefix 'The') was later given to 'Deltic' (Class 55) D9013 in January 1963.

▲ On its way back home to Bolton after overhaul at Cowlairs Works 'Black Five' 4-6-0 No. 45312 was spotted at Corkerhill on March 29, 1964. One of a batch built by Armstrong Whitworth in 1937 this loco survived until the very last months of steam on BR, being withdrawn from Bolton shed (26C) in June 1968.

▶ My visit to Corkerhill shed on 29 March 1964 revealed some absolute corkers! In amongst the many BR Standards and 'Black 5s' were three 'Royal Scot' Nos. 46102, 46104 and 46162 (all stored out of use at the back of the shed) along with 'Jubilee' No. 45608.

45178	80050	73077
45356	76099	80127
D8507	76098	80049
42126	76094	45366
D8502	73101	80046
42125	73102	45171
D8546	76001	76093
42169	80047	76091
D8550	80008	45608
45468	73123	73005
44787	76092	46162
67A	80030	46993
D3923	80005	D2438
D2442	73121	D2443
73124	76095	46102
D14	80044	46104
D18	42196	44786
80128	45312	45251
44791	80021	D2440
80025	73120	D3924
17M	27ST	9D

Edinburgh Princes Street

With its two city-centre stations, four engine sheds and two sub-sheds, Edinburgh was well-worth visiting for a trainspotting bash in the early 1960s. The two stations, Waverley and Princes Street, were only a short distance apart along Princes Street, but there the similarity ends.

Originally opened in 1870, Princes Street station was the Edinburgh terminus of the Caledonian Railway. By 1893 it had been rebuilt and enlarged as a grand Victorian station with seven platforms and an adjoining hotel. For years it provided long-distance services to London via Carstairs (also served by local services until 1964) and the West Coast Main Line and local services to the north and west of the city and to Glasgow via Shotts. Sleeper trains also departed from Princes Street every evening – although by Summer 1964 this was down to just one with portions for Birmingham, Liverpool (Lime Street) and Manchester (Exchange) departing at 23.30 on most nights.

Motive power as far as Carstairs was normally provided by ex-LMS locos such as 'Black Five' 4-6-0s from nearby Dalry Road shed (64C). Services from Princes Street were gradually run down during the early 1960s and it was closed in 1965. Sadly this grand Victorian edifice was demolished but travellers can still enjoy the Caledonian Railway's grand hotel now renamed Caledonian Hilton.

▶ Not far from Princes Street station was Dalry Road shed. Seen on a visit on 29 March 1964 were some interesting occupants including three stored locomotives awaiting their fate – 'A4' Nos. 60006 and 60007 and ex-Caledonian Railway Class '2P' 0-4-4T No. 55189. Of these, 60007 'Sir Nigel Gresley and No. 55189 were fortunately preserved but No. 60006 'Sir Ralph Wedgwood' was not so lucky and was withdrawn in September 1965.

▼ Despite its local stopping train headlamps, Stanier 'Black 5' 4-6-0 No. 45173 seems to have a Royal Mail Travelling Post Office coach also in trail. The date is May 1964 and Princes Street station and taxi concourse looks eerily quiet. A Carstairs loco, the 'Black 5' was withdrawn only two months later.

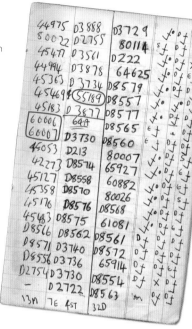

◄ Fairburn Class '4' 2-6-4T No. 42271 arrives at Princes Street station with a local stopping train on 8 May 1963. For many years allocated to nearby Dalry Road shed, this loco spent its last years at Leeds Holbeck before withdrawal at the end of 1966.

▶ Headed by a Stanier 'Black 5', a four-coach train to Carstairs and Lanark waits for passengers to board at Edinburgh Princes Street station shortly before closure in 1965.

▲ A three-car Cross-Country dmu waits to depart from Princes street station with a train for Glasgow Central via Shotts on 30 August 1965. Listed for closure in the 'Beeching Report', this route was subsequently reprieved although Princes Street closed just one week after this photo was taken.

Edinburgh Waverley

Just a short distance down Princes Street is the second largest station in the UK – Edinburgh Waverley. Located in a valley formed by a drained loch, the station was built by the North British Railway in 1866 on the site of three smaller stations. It was enlarged after the opening of the Forth Bridge and rebuilt as a 19-platform terminus and through station in 1902.

W averley has always been a popular station with railway photographers due to the panoramic view of it afforded from North Bridge. It was also popular with trainspotters because of the wide variety of ex-LNER locos to be seen and the diverse destinations served. These ranged from trains to Glasgow Queen Street including the luxury 'Queen of Scots Pullman' and Gresley 'A4' Pacifics from Haymarket shed on romantically named East Coast Main Line expresses such as 'The Flying Scotsman', 'The Elizabethan' and 'The Talisman', to 'A1' and 'A2' Pacifics on trains to Dundee and Aberdeen and 'A3' Pacifics on Waverley Route trains, such as 'The Waverley' to London St Pancras, via Carlisle.

However, by 1963 Haymarket shed had become a diesel depot and ECML expresses were headed by English Electric Type 4 (Class 40) or 'Deltic' diesels (Class 55) from the nearby Haymarket shed (64B), Waverley Route trains were headed by 'Peaks' (Class 45/46) and services to the north were often in the hands of Birmingham R. C. & W. Type 2 diesels (Class 27). Steam became rarer and rarer until May 1967 when the remaining steam shed in Edinburgh, St Margarets (64B), was closed. Amidst much public consternation, the Waverley Route closed in 1969.

HST sets replaced the 'Deltics' in the late 1970s and these, in turn, were superseded by InterCity 225 trains when electrification of the ECML to King's Cross was completed in 1990.

▲ Eastfield's Class 'B1' 4-6-0 No. 61140 running with a self-weighing tender enters Edinburgh Waverley station with an express from Glasgow Queen Street on 31 August 1956.

▲ A panoramic view of Waverley in August 1958 that is certain to please both the train and bus spotter.

▶ In the final year of operation of this famous train, 'A4' Pacific No. 60014 'Silver Link' leaves Waverley with the up 'Elizabethan' non-stop express to King's Cross on August 20, 1961. Built in 1935, this loco was the first of its class and was withdrawn from King's Cross shed (34A) at the end of 1962. Some 'A4s' were fitted with corridor tenders to enable a crew-change on this non-stop service.

◀ During the final months of steam at Waverley, 'Black Five' No. 44954, allocated to Carstairs shed (66E), gets ready to depart with a parcels train on July 29, 1966. This loco was built at Horwich in 1946 and withdrawn at the end of September 1966.

Edinburgh St Margarets

64 A

A dangerous shed to visit, as it was located on both sides of the main line about 1½ miles east of Waverley station. The original round house at St Margarets was built on the north side of the line by the North British Railway in 1846. Part of the old building was later used for the stabling of smaller steam locomotives.

Although the shed foreman's office was on the north side, the main shed, opened by the NBR in 1866, was located on the south side of the line and using the boarded crossing over the main line could be a perilous matter. Even in October 1961 the rather antiquated and run down St Margarets had a large allocation of mixed-traffic, freight and shunting steam locos on the south site while there were 44 diesel shunters stabled on the north site. The steam tally totalled 134 locos with representatives from 12 different classes including six classes of vintage North British Railway locos. The oldest of these were the seven 'J36' 0-6-0s dating from 1888 including one named example (65224 'Mons'). Other NBR types were 'J35', 'J37', 'J88', 'J83', and 'N15'. Ex-LNER

▲ Built by BR at Doncaster in 1948, Peppercorn Class 'A2' Pacific No. 60534 'Irish Elegance' simmers away nicely in the yard at Edinburgh St Margarets in August 1962 just four months before her final withdrawal from service in December of that year.

mixed traffic locos totalled 52 of which 28 were 'V2' 2-6-2s and 24 were 'B1' 4-6-0s including five named examples. St Margaret's also housed three 'A3' and four 'A2' Pacifics.

A visit to the shed on a weekday in early August 1964 revealed 50 steam locos, six main line diesels, five diesel shunters and seven Clayton Type 1 (Class 17). After the closure of Haymarket (64B) to steam in 1963, St Margarets received a few 'A4' and more 'A3' Pacifics that had been made redundant from that shed. One of the last steam sheds in Scotland it was finally closed down in May 1967.

▶ With Birmingham R.C. & W. Co Type 2 diesel D5304 in the background, local boy ex-LMS 'Black Five' 4-6-0 No. 45162 and visiting ex-LNER Class 'V2' 2-6-2 No. 60836 make a fine sight outside St Margarets on 24 April, 1966. The 'Black Five' was built by Armstrong Whitworth in 1935 and withdrawn from St Margarets in November 1966. The 'V2' was built at Darlington in 1938 and withdrawn from Dundee Tay Bridge (62B) at the end of 1966.

A much-photographed celebrity by this time, 'A4' Pacific No. 60024 'Kingfisher' looks a magnificent sight on the turntable at St Margarets in September 1966. This beautiful engine was withdrawn within a few days of this photograph being taken and was cut-up five months later in a miserable North Blyth scrapyard.

D9019	65919	D265
D8554	60955	80114
D2753	60152	80003
D8558	46462	61344
D2755	65920	60813
D9016	65914	60041
D3560	61324	60457
D2728	61397	60084
D181	80007	60085
64A	44704	65915
61245	61308	65939
80022	61354	
60147	61404	60112
60001	61076	65912
80054	60970	61029
80026	60127	61350
60129	61294	76049
80086	45309	60042
80055	42691	60077
60051	80122	60882
25T 12E	69128	D390
		3D

After visiting Haymarket shed on August 2, 1964 (see pages 176-7), I went over to St Margarets shed where there was still an abundance of active ex-LNER locos. For a trainspotter from Gloucester this was heaven - included in the line up was 'A4' No. 60007 (rescued from storage at Dalry Road - see page 170), six 'A3s', five 'A1s', four 'V2s' and eleven 'B1's and there were even more on my next notebook page!

Gresley's 'A3's were every bit as graceful as the famous racehorses they were named after, and their scintillating performances over the East Coast Main Line truly lived up to the association. In later years, the 'A3's acquired double chimneys and German style smoke deflectors, modifications which - although imposing - greatly marred their original beauty. Here, complete with German style smoke deflectors, is No.60041 'Salmon Trout' at St Margarets shortly before withdrawal in 1965.

Edinburgh Haymarket

64 B

Although there had been an engine shed at Haymarket since 1848, the building so loved by trainspotters in the 1950s and early '60s was built by the North British Railway in 1894. The shed came under the control of the newly-formed LNER following the 1923 Grouping and mainly provided top link locos for East Coast Main Line trains out of Edinburgh Waverley station. It was located on the north side of the line about a 10-minute walk west of Haymarket station and with its very large allocation of ex-LNER Pacifics Haymarket was a magnet for trainspotters. However, by the early 1960s, its days as a steam shed were definitely numbered.

With the influx of English Electric Type 4 (Class 40) and 'Deltic' (Class 55) diesels, by October 1961 its steam allocation had been reduced to 41 locos of which seven were 'A4', 11 were 'A3', five were 'A1' and three 'A2' Pacifics. Thrown in for good measure were some old timers whose lives were about to be cut short such as two named 'D11' 4-4-0s (62691 'Laird of Balmawhapple' and 62693 'Roderick Dhu') and two named 1891-vintage NBR 'J36' 0-6-0s (65235 'Gough' and 65243 'Maude'). At the same time its diesel allocation included 14 English Electric Type 4 (Class 40), 19 Birmingham

▲ *A visitor to Haymarket from Heaton (52B) gets ready for a trip home down the ECML from Edinburgh. Thompson Class A2/3 4-6-2 No. 60511 'Airborne' was built at Doncaster in 1946 and withdrawn from Tweedmouth shed (52D) in October 1962.*

R. C. & W. Type 2 and five of the brand new 'Deltic' diesels (Class 55).

Haymarket closed to steam in September 1963 with many of its Pacifics being transferred to other Scottish locations such as St Margarets, Aberdeen Ferryhill and Dundee Tay Bridge. A visit to Haymarket at the end of July 1964 revealed 30 diesels including three 'Deltic', six English Electric Type 4, six Birmingham R. C. & W. Type 2, one of the first Brush Type 4 D1507 (Class 47) and ten of the later batch of the highly unsuccessful Clayton Type 1 (Class 17) diesels. The shed continues in use as a diesel maintenance depot.

▼ *Photographed on 1 May, 1954, examples of ex-LNER Classes 'A3' 4-6-2, 'B1' 4-6-0 and 'V2' 2-6-2 line up outside Haymarket in the days when steam reigned supreme.*

▲ Ex-LNER Class 'A3' Pacific No. 60035 'Windsor Lad' looks immaculate in this photo taken at Haymarket in the late 1950s. Built at Doncaster in 1934 and spending much of its life allocated to 64B, No. 60035 was withdrawn in September 1961 and was cut up at its birthplace one month later.

▼ 100% diesel since September 1963, Edinburgh Haymarket shed had a varied collection of locos recorded during my visit on 2 August 1964 - along with Birminghanm Railway Carriage & Wagon Company Type 2s, Peaks, English Electric Type 4s and a couple of 'Deltics', those appalling Clayton Type 1s were also in evidence. In 1964 they were nearly brand new but had all been withdrawn by 1971.

D8576	D5301	08571	X X
D8570	D5306	D260	X X X
45360	D5364	D361	X X
45009	D173	D1583	X X X
45155	D5308	D266	X X
45127	D5311	D367	X X
73056	D5307	D357	X X
42273	D5302	D366	X X
44994	D5303	D5117	X X
45469	D5314	D8563	X X
45053	D5310	D22	X X
45011	08573	D3738	X X
45161	D5304	D5317	X X
44975	08562	D9021	X X
D2754	D364	08557	X X X
45168	D8575	D1501	X X X
61307	D8564	D8555	X X X
61351	08579	D9013	X X
648	D8580	D2751	— X
D167	D262	D2752	X X
	1M	9D	

◀ Two unkempt Peppercorn Class 'A1' Pacifics line up for duty at Haymarket on 6 October, 1962. On the left is No. 60155 'Borderer', then allocated to Heaton (52B), built by BR in 1949 at Doncaster and withdrawn from York (50A) in October 1965. Behind it is No. 60161 'North British', then allocated to 64B, built by BR at Doncaster at the end of 1949 and withdrawn from St Margarets (64A) in October 1963 - a short life of less than 14 years for such a fine machine. In contrast the NBL 0-4-0 diesel shunter, D2753, was one of three such machines allocated to Haymarket at that time.

ON SHED

Thornton Junction

62 A

▼ Ex-LNER 'B1' Class 4-6-0 No. 61147 was spotted at Thornton shed during a visit on 30 July, 1964. It was built by Vulcan Foundry in 1947 and withdrawn from Dundee Tay Bridge (62B) at the end of 1965. Behind the 'B1' is a Class 'J37' 0-6-0 minus its centre driving wheel and connecting rod.

The main engine shed for the former North British Railway and LNER in this coal-mining region of Fife, Thornton Junction's allocation included a large number of heavy-freight and mixed traffic locos. Located on the south side of the Thornton to Dunfermline line, the shed was a good 25-minute walk from the little station at Thornton Junction. The final building on this site was a seven-road through shed opened by the LNER in 1933 and by October 1961 it had an allocation of 52 steam locos and 16 diesel shunters. The mainstay of the motive power was provided by 12 'B1' 4-6-0s, 15 'J38' and eight ex-NBR 'J37' 0-6-0s and 12 ex-WD 2-8-0s. The last surviving 'K4' 2-6-0 No. 61994 'The Great Marquess', built by the LNER for working on the West Highland line, was also allocated to Thornton at this time just prior to withdrawal and preservation.

A visit to the shed at the end of August 1964 revealed 40 steam locos and seven diesel shunters. Even on a visit in late August 1966 our spotter found 14 steam locos and five diesel shunters along with English Electric Type 3 (Class 37) D6859. By then these handsome engines were becoming seen in increasing numbers along with the Brush Type 4 (Class 47) diesels.

Its sub-sheds were at Anstruther (closed 1960), Burntisland (closed 1958), Kirkcaldy (closed 1959), Ladybank (closed 1958) and Methil (closed 1958). Thornton Junction shed closed completely in April 1967.

◀ Apart from seven diesel shunters Thornton Junction shed was 100% steam on July 30, 1964. Amongst those seen were ex-WD 2-8-0 and J37, J38 and ancient ex-NBR J36 0-6-0 freight locos, Nos. 65345 and 65287.

▶ Allocated to Thornton Junction, ex-NBR Class 'J37' 0-6-0 No. 64570 seems to have received some cosmetic treatment to its front end when photographed at the shed by Colin Garratt in 1965. Introduced in 1914, the final survivors of this class survived until the end of steam in Scotland in 1967.

Dundee Tay Bridge

62 B

► One of three such locos allocated to Tay Bridge at this time, Peppercorn Class 'A2' Pacific No. 60528 'Tudor Minstrel' looks in fine fettle on 30 September, 1965. Built by BR at Doncaster in 1948 'Tudor Minstrel' was withdrawn from Aberdeen Ferryhill in June 1966. Another ex-62B 'A2', No. 60532 "Blue Peter' was later saved for preservation.

◄ Dundee Tay Bridge shed on September 1, 1954. In the foreground on the turntable is ex-NBR Class 'J35/4' No. 64492, while in the background is an unidentified Class 'V2' 2-6-2. A total of 70 of the Class 'J35' locos were built between 1906 and 1913 by the North British Locomotive Company and at the NBR Cowlairs Works. Used for coal traffic and pick-up goods, the last of the class was withdrawn from service in 1962.

► Dundee Tay Bridge shed on July 30, 1964. On shed that day were the two local stars, 'A2' Pacifics Nos 60532 'Blue Peter' and 60528 'Tudor Minstrel' and 'A4' Pacific No. 60012 'Commonwealth of Australia'. The latter loco was withdrawn from Ferryhill shed (61B) three weeks later.

Up until 1958 there were two steam sheds in Dundee – Dundee West, opened by the Caledonian Railway in 1885, and Dundee Tay Bridge, opened by the North British Railway in 1878. The former was closed in 1958 and used as a diesel depot and for storage of withdrawn steam locos. Tay Bridge, located on the north side of the line a short distance west of Dundee Tay Bridge station, was an eight-road through shed with an allocation of 35 steam locos in October 1961.

A visit to the shed in early August 1964 revealed 28 steam locos including five 'V2' 2-6-2s and ten 'B1' 4-6-0s with two familiar local stars – 'A2' Pacifics No. 60532 'Blue Peter' (since preserved) and No. 60528 'Tudor Minstrel' – and 'A4' Pacific No. 60012 'Commonwealth of Australia'. At the same time West shed had four stored steam locos (two 'B1's and two 'V2's) and 11 diesels (of which nine were shunters). Tay Bridge shed finally closed in May 1967.

Perth

The Gateway to the Highlands,
Perth was, and still is, an
important railway junction.
It was here that the Highland
Railway from Inverness
met the Caledonian Railway
from Glasgow, Aberdeen and
Dundee and the North British
Railway from Edinburgh.

Sadly, the former CR lines to Lochearnhead via Crieff (closed 1964)
and to Kinnaber Junction via Forfar (closed 1967) have now gone.
The Highland line became the first casualty of dieselisation and by
1962 all trains previously hauled by 'Black Five' 4-6-0s to Inverness were in
the hands of the Birmingham R. C. & W. Type 2 (Class 27) and BR Sulzer
Type 2 (Class 24) diesels.

On a journey from Perth to Inverness in late July 1964 our trainspotter
travelled in a 14-coach train double-headed by D5327 and D5127. By
then Inverness shed was 100% diesel and the return journey was on a
16-coach train double-headed by D5115 and D5124.

Until the Autumn of 1966 the highlights of a day's trainspotting at
Perth were the Glasgow to Aberdeen three-hour expresses which, since
1962, were usually headed by one of Aberdeen Ferryhill's 'A4' Pacifics,
reallocated there after the dieselisation of the ECML. Other classes
regularly seen at Perth included Polmadie's (66A) BR 'Clan' Pacifics and
'Jubilee' and 'Royal Scot' 4-6-0s often seen at the head of the West Coast
Postal or on overnight fish trains, and other local services in the hands of
'Black Five' and BR Standard Class 5 4-6-0s.

◄ Halting under an old Caledonian Railway bracket signal, rather grimy ex-LMS 'Royal Scot' 4-6-0 No. 46166 'London Rifle Brigade' arrives at Perth with a down express in May 1959. Glistening in the low evening sunshine 'Black Five' 4-6-0 No. 44997 waits to take over the train. The 'Royal Scot' was built in 1930, rebuilt with a taper boiler in 1945 and withdrawn in September 1964. The 'Black Five' was built at Horwich in 1947 and withdrawn from Perth shed (63A) in May 1967.

▶ Stanier 'Black 5' 4-6-0 No. 44994 blows off steam at Perth station on 4 August 1963 while two earnest trainspotters try to have a decent conversation. The loco was withdrawn from Dalry Road shed (64C) a year later.

▶ Having deputised for failed 'A4' No. 60034 'Lord Faringdon' at Forfar, 'A4' No. 60009 'Union of South Africa', allocated to Ferryhill (61B) calls at Perth with the 7.10am train from Aberdeen to Glasgow on 29 September, 1965. No. 60009 was built in 1937, withdrawn in June 1966 and has since been preserved. Originally named 'Peregrine', No. 60034 was built in 1938 and withdrawn in August 1966.

◄ Class 'A4' 4-6-2 No. 60019 'Bittern' receives admiring glances at Perth while heading an Aberdeen to Glasgow express on 31 August, 1964. 'Bittern' was built at Doncaster in 1937, withdrawn from Ferryhill shed (61B) in September 1966 and has since been preserved.

Perth 63 A

► *St Rollox's BR Standard Caprotti Class 5 4-6-0 No. 73147 stands in all its glory on the turntable at Perth shed in the late 1950s. Marvellous locomotives and to think this one was scrapped after only 8½ years service to make way for those dreadful NBL Type 2s!*

Perth South shed was opened by the Caledonian Railway in the mid-19th century and was replaced by a new eight-road through shed by the LMS in 1938. The shed was located on the west side of the main line about a 15-minute walk south from Perth station. Its allocation in the 1950s included many ageing Caledonian Railway locos and a large number of 'Black Five' 4-6-0s, used in multiple for working heavily-loaded trains on the Highland line to Inverness. The shed also supplied motive power for trains on the former CR routes to Crieff, Dundee and Aberdeen via Forfar.

By October 1961 its allocation totalled 55 steam locos made up of eight different classes, including a dwindling number of ex-CR types, the oldest of

which was a solitary Drummnd 2F 0-6-0 (No. 57345) dating from 1892. By far the largest contingent were the 35 'Black Fives' although, by now, their numbers were dwindling due to dieselisation of the Highland line by a fleet of 27 Birmingham R. C. & W Type 2 diesels (Class 27) based at Inverness. A visit to Perth shed at the end of July 1964 revealed just 24 steam locos (and eight diesels) including 'Royal Scot' No. 46128, 'Jubilee' No. 45629, 'B1' No. 61294 and a solitary CR 2P 0-4-4 tank, No. 55204.

Perth had four sub-sheds – Aberfeldy (closed 1962), Blair Atholl (closed 1962), Forfar (closed 1964) and Crieff (closed 1958). Perth shed closed to steam in May 1967 but continued as a diesel depot until 1969.

◄ *Perth shed was visited on July 30, 1964 and of the 32 locos spotted 24 were steam. Visiting from Carlisle Kingmoor (12A) was 'Royal Scot' Class 4-6-0 No. 46128 'The Lovat Scouts'. This loco was withdrawn in May the following year.*

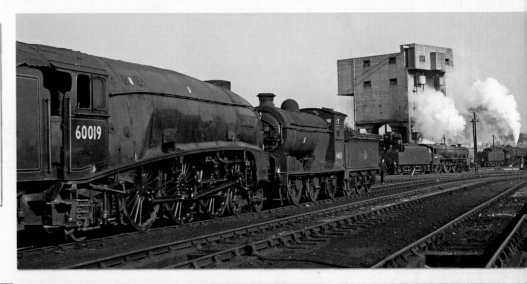

◀ Not far from home, one of Dundee Tay Bridge shed's Peppercorn 'A2' Class Pacifics, No. 60528 'Tudor Minstrel' was spotted visiting Perth shed on 11 January, 1962. Named after the racehorse that won the '2000 Guineas' in 1947 and built by the infant BR at Doncaster early in 1948, this loco was withdrawn from Ferryhill (61B) in June 1966.

▼ In the 1950s Perth was home to around 70 Stanier 'Black Fives'. Dieselisation of the Highland main line had vastly reduced their numbers but even on July 30, 1964 there were still 16 to be seen on shed. Although withdrawn over 18 months previously ex-Caledonian Railway McIntosh 0-4-4 tank No. 55204 was still languishing there.

◀ Gavin Morrison's photo of Perth Shed on 13 August 1965 - left to right: 'A4' Class 4-6-2 No. 60019 'Bittern' (since preserved); ex-NBR Class 'J37' 0-6-0 No. 64621; Stanier 'Black 5' 4-6-0 No. 45473; BR 'Britannia' Class 4-6-2 No. 70038 'Robin Hood'.

▲ Even the rays of the evening sunshine fail to add any glamour to decrepit 'A4' Pacific No. 60031 'Golden Plover' as it awaits its fate outside Perth shed on 28 August, 1965. Built at Doncaster in 1937 'Golden Plover' was the sole 'A4' allocated to St Rollox shed (65B) in 1965 and was withdrawn in November of that year.

Aberdeen Kittybrewster

The first shed at Kittybrewster was built by the Great North of Scotland Railway in the mid-19th century. This was replaced at a later date by a half-roundhouse and was modified by BR in 1956. The shed was located two miles northwest of Aberdeen on the west side of the Inverness main line, only about a five-minute walk from Kittybrewster station.

Until closure to steam, the shed, which provided motive power for all of the GNoSR routes north and west of Aberdeen, was famed for its wondrous collection of veteran steam locos from pre-Grouping railway companies including the North Eastern Railway, Great North of Scotland Railway and the Great Eastern Railway plus other ex-LNER and ex-LMS types.

By October 1961 it had lost its steam allocation entirely and had 44 diesels on its books including nine Barclay 0-4-0 shunters for working around Aberdeen Docks, 15 0-6-0 shunters and the final 20 of the luckless North British Type 2 (Class 21). Despite this, on a visit to the shed at the end of July 1964 one lucky spotter found 'A4' Pacific No. 60007 'Sir Nigel Gresley' in store prior to its later preservation.

Sub-sheds were at Ballater (closed 1958), Fraserburgh (closed 1961), Inverurie (closed 1959) and Peterhead (closed 1965). Kittybrewster closed to steam in 1961 but was retained as a diesel depot for a while.

▼ One of only two Class 'Z5' 0-4-2 tanks built for the North British Railway by Manning Wardle in 1915, No. 68192 awaits its fate in the scrap line at Kittybrewster in May 1960. These diminutive locos were built for shunting duties in Aberdeen Docks. To the right veteran ex-NBR Class 'J36' 0-6-0 No. 65247 similarly awaits its fate.

► Kittybrewster and Ferryhill sheds were visited on July 31, 1964. The train from Glasgow Buchanan St was headed by D5368 and three 'A4' Pacifics, Nos 60009, 60027, 60034, were spotted en route.

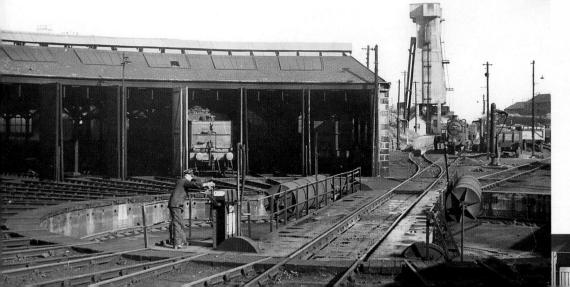

◄ Seen here in 1954, the former GNoSR semi-roundhouse at Kittybrewster was home to an amazing assortment of veteran pre-Grouping steam locos. In the distance an unidentified 0-6-0 tender loco prepares to move down to the turntable.

► *Although famous for its allocation of 'A4' Pacifics in 1964, other, more mundane, steam classes could also be seen in action at Ferryhill. Here, on March 20, are BR Standard Class 4 2-6-4 tank No. 80055, ex-works Class 'J37' 0-6-0 No. 64620 and ex-WD 2-8-0 No. 90705. No. 80055 was built at Derby in 1954 and withdrawn from St Margarets (64A) in September 1966. The 'J37', an ex-NBR design introduced in 1914, was one of the final three that were withdrawn from Dundee Tay Bridge (62B) in April 1967. The 'DubDee' was withdrawn from Thornton Junction (62A) only four months after photographed here.*

Operated jointly by the North British and Caledonian Railways, the 10-road shed at Ferryhill opened in 1908 and provided motive power for main line services south of Aberdeen to Glasgow via Forfar and Perth and to Edinburgh via Dundee.

The shed was located on the west side of the main line south of the junction with the Dee Valley line to Ballater, and was only a short walk from Aberdeen station. Following the dieselisation of the East Coast Main Line in 1962, the shed was allocated displaced Gresley 'A4' Pacifics to operate the three-hour expresses to Glasgow via Forfar and Perth. During their swan song, these fine locos put up sterling performances until the Autumn of 1966, when all of these trains became diesel-hauled and were diverted via the Dundee route.

A visit to Ferryhill at the end of July 1964 revealed 21 locos of which only three were diesels including English Electric Type 4 (Class 40) D362. On the plus side our trainspotter noted in his excitement that there were seven 'A4' Pacifics (No. 60004 'William Whitelaw', No. 60006 'Sir Ralph Wedgwood', No. 60010 'Dominion of Canada', No. 60012 'Commonwealth of Australia', No. 60016 'Silver King', No. 60023 'Golden Eagle' and No. 60026 'Miles Beevor') on shed. A ride back to Glasgow Buchanan Street behind No. 60019 'Bittern' was a fitting end to this blissful day! No. 60024 'Kingfisher' repeated this treat in late August 1966. Ferryhill shed closed to steam in March 1967.

► *Ferryhill shed on July 31, 1964 was a wondrous place - on shed that day were no less than seven 'A4' Pacifics, relegated there after the dieselisation of the ECML. The trip back to Buchanan St. was behind No. 60019 making it the twelfth 'A4' seen that day.*

▼ *One of the seven 'A4' Pacifics seen at Ferryhill on July 31, 1964 was No. 60026 'Miles Beevor'. Employed on the three-hour Aberdeen to Glasgow expresses, the 'Streaks' performed their swansong until September 1966. Built at Doncaster in 1937 and previously allocated to King's Cross (34A) 'Miles Beevor' was finally withdrawn at the end of 1965.*

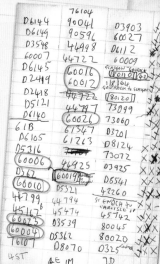

Index

About the Author

Author and photographer **Julian Holland** spent his formative years, notebook and camera in hand, trainspotting on draughty stations and in grimy engine sheds and travelling the highways and byways of the British Railways network in search of that elusive locomotive number or to travel over a soon-to-be-closed line. The repercussions of the 'Beeching Report' and the end of steam on British Railways in 1968 failed to dampen his passion for railways –as benign dictator of the UK he would now renationalise the railway system and reopen many of the long-closed railway lines!

Trained as a graphic designer at the infamous Hornsey College of Art in the late '60s, Julian went on to a successful career creating books for many well-known publishing companies. In more recent years he has contributed to many best-selling books on railways and has also written *Amazing and Extraordinary Railway Facts* (David & Charles 2007), *Discovering Britain's Little Trains* (AA Publishing 2008), *Great Railways of the World* (AA Publishing 2008), *The Lost Joy of Railways* (David & Charles 2009), *More Amazing and Extraordinary Railway Facts* (David & Charles 2010), *Amazing & Extraordinary Facts: Trains & Railways* (David & Charles 2011), *The Times Mapping the Railways* (Times Books 2011), *Amazing & Extraordinary Facts: The Steam Age* (David & Charles 2012), *Railway Days Out* (AA Publishing 2012) and *The Times Britain's Scenic Railways* (Times Books 2012).

As a writer and photographer he has also produced *Water Under the Bridge* (Collins & Brown 1998), *Exploring the Islands of England and Wales* (Frances Lincoln 2007) and *Exploring the Islands of Scotland* (Frances Lincoln 2008).

Acknowledgments

Firstly I would like to thank my late mother, Joan, for squirreling away my trainspotting books in her loft for 33 years – without this unique material this book would not have been possible. Thanks are also due to all of the railway photographers out there – in particular Ben Ashworth, John Goss, Tony Harden, Tom Heavyside, Alan Jarvis and Michael Mensing – and to Ron White of Colour-Rail who have supplied many of the photographs used in this book and to David & Charles for use of their photographic archive.

I am especially grateful to those employees of British Railways who put up with our antics during those 'golden years' – they must have thought the younger generation had gone completely mad! For their companionship I would also like to thank my old trainspotting friends in Gloucester – I am sorry I cannot remember all your names after all this time – and to Robert Meadows with whom I spent many happy weekends and holidays operating his garden railway. Last but not least thanks are also due to Peter Hughes, formerly of Gourock in Scotland, with whom I spent many happy hours 'bunking' engine sheds and travelling around the highways and byways of the Scottish Region in the 1960s. Peter now lives in Vancouver and made contact once again (via David & Charles) after buying *The Lost Joy of Railways* in 2011.

Finally I would like to thank David & Charles, publishers of this book, who were brave enough to let me off the leash on such a large project.

Picture credits

Unless otherwise credited all ephemera and notebook pages are from the author's collection.

l = left; r = right; m = middle; b = bottom; t = top

D A Anderson: 129tr; 177tl
B J Ashworth: 7; 8tl; 14tr; 15tr; 15mr; 17br; 22/23t; 23br; 27b; 33tl; 44bl; 45bl; 45br; 47bl; 49tl; 65tl; 68br; 69bl; 107bl; 107tr; 117tl; 137b; 149
D H Ballantyne: 48tr; 67tr; 67b
Peter Bowles: 71tl
British Railways: 31bl
Melvyn Bryan: 109bl; 165tr
D. E. Canning: 75ml
I S Carr: 148tr
Jim Carter: 127bl
H C Casserley: 136tr; 138bl; 140tr; 154tr; 154ml; 154br
C R L Coles: 58tr; 76tr; 121tr
Colour-Rail: title page; 8br; 10t; 11br; 14bl; 18mr; 19tr; 19bl; 20tr; 22br; 25t; 27tr; 29tl; 47tl; 48bl; 56tr; 68tr; 73tl; 77tl; 79; 81tl; 82tr; 84mr; 85bl; 88b; 90br; 91tl; 92; 93b; 97t; 99t; 99bl; 103br; 107tl; 109tl; 115t; 116tr; 128br; 131tl; 133tr; 133bl; 141tl; 142br; 143tl; 145tl; 147mr; 151b; 152br; 155mr; 155bl; 158tr; 159; 161br; 163br; 165bl; 168bl; 170b; 171tl; 171bl; 171br; 173t; 174tr; 175tl; 177bl; 180tr; 181tr; 182tr; 183bl; 184tr
K Connolly: 31br; 53bl; 130br; 139br
S Creer: 102br; 120tr
C E Dann: 81br
M Dunnett: 80tr; 130tr; 143b; 144bl; 146ml
Mike Esau: 20br; 57tr; 59tl; 60tr; 61br; 63tl; 83t; 83bl; 97br; 101tl; 102tr; 109br; 118br; 119bl
J N Faulkner: 122tr
Kenneth Field: 56br; 110ml; 111bl; 120br; 123bl; 136br; 138br
J A Fleming: 104tr; 104b; 105t; 113t; 115br
P R Foster: 143ml; 145bl
John Goss: 21tl; 21mr; 23tr; 24bl; 28tr; 28br; 29ml; 32br; 37mr; 37bl; 42tr; 44tr; 57b; 66tr; 70tr; 70br; 73br; 78tr; 90tr; 96tr; 96br; 101ml; 101br; 105bl; 132br; 139tr; 139ml; 140b; 147tl; 150ml; 151tl; 153tl; 153br; 160tr; 162br; 165tl; 166tr; 172br; 176tr; 179tr; 181br; 183tl
R M Grainger: 55ml; 63bl; 87tr

Tony Harden: 24tr; 64bl; 86bl; 98tr; 119tl; 119mr; 132tr; 146br; 157ml; 157br; 164tr; 166br; 167t; 168tr; 176b; 179ml; 184bl
Tom Heavyside: 50tr; 50br; 52tr; 52bl; 53tl; 55br; 58br; 59mr; 62tr; 65mr; 65b; 66br; 86bl; 95br; 116br; 117bl; 125mr; 128tr; 129l; 138tr; 141b; 155t; 185tr
G F Heiron: 46br
Julian Holland: 6tl; 6mr; 9tr; 9br; 25tl; 32tr; 40tr; 40br; 41tr; 41m; 41br; 43tl; 69tr; 72tr; 72br; 113br; 162tr; 164ml; 169tl; 169tr; 169bl; 178tr; 180br; 185br
Peter Hughes: 9ml
Alan Jarvis: 17ml; 34tr; 34b; 35t; 35bl; 36br; 38tr; 38bl; 38br; 39tr; 39mr; 39br; 42br; 44br; 45tr; 61tl; 63br
M C Kemp: 129br
Michael Mensing: 26tr; 26br; 75br; 77bl; 106tr; 106br; 108tr; 108br; 125tl
Milepost 92½: 12b; 13tl; 30tl; 36tl; 37br; 82br; 87b; 88tr; 89tr; 89bl; 93tr; 111tl; 112tr; 112br; 118tr; 121bl; 122br; 124bl; 126b; 144tr; 147bl; 148tr; 152tr; 174tr; 175bl; 178br
R Montgomery: 80br
Brian Morrison: 18tr; 103tl
Gavin Morrison: 33bl; 43bl; 85t; 100tr; 124tl; 142tr; 150tr; 158b; 161tl; 163tr; 172tr; 182br
John K Morton: 71br; 84tr; 123tl; 123mr; 137tr; 143br; 145mr
Barry J Nicolle: 21bl
Ivo Peters Collection: 31tr
R F Roberts: 131bl
Gerald T Robinson: 51br
D Trevor Rowe: 95ml;100br
W S Sellar: 173br
John R Smith: 46tr
R Smith: 127tr
Rev Graham B Wise: 114

Ordnance survey maps originally published by David & Charles.

A DAVID & CHARLES BOOK

A DAVID & CHARLES BOOK
© F&W Media International, Ltd 2012

David & Charles is an imprint of F&W Media International, Ltd
Brunel House, Forde Close, Newton Abbot, TQ12 4PU, UK

F&W Media International, Ltd is a subsidiary of F+W Media, Inc
10151 Carver Road, Suite #200, Blue Ash, OH 45242, USA

First published in the UK in 2012

Text copyright ©Julian Holland 2012
Photographs copyright © see page 191

Julian Holland has asserted his right to be identified as author of this work in accordance with the Copyright, Designs and Patents Act, 1988.

Some material in this publication was originally published in *The Lost Joy of Railways*, 2009

A catalogue record for this book is available from the British Library.

ISBN-13: 978-1-4463-0262-0
ISBN-10: 1-4463-0262-8

Printed in China by R.R. Donnelley for F&W Media International, Brunel House, Newton Abbot, Devon

Trade Community Leader Judith Harvey
Editor Verity Graves-Morris
Designer Sue Cleave
Senior Designer Victoria Marks
Production Manager Beverley Richardson

F+W Media publish high quality books on a wide range of subjects.
For more great book titles visit: **www.fwmedia.co.uk**

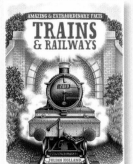
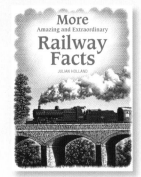
LOVED THIS BOOK?

Tell us what you think and you could win another fantastic book from David & Charles in our monthly prize draw.

www.lovethisbook.co.uk

Watching the trains go by – a lone trainspotter watches as ex-works unrebuilt 'Patriot' Class No. 45503 'The Royal Leicestershire Regiment' restarts a mixed goods train near Hartford station, south of Weaver Junction, on February 17, 1952. Built at Crewe in 1932, the 'Pat' was withdrawn from Carlisle Upperby in August 1961.